THE
CRISIS
IN
EDUCATION

RHODES BOYSON, M.P.

THE WOBURN PRESS

First published 1975 in Great Britain by
THE WOBURN PRESS
67 Great Russell Street,
London WC1B 3BT, England

Copyright © 1975 Rhodes Boyson

ISBN 0 7130 0142 9 (Case)
ISBN 0 7130 4001 7 (Paper)

Made and printed in Great Britain by
The Garden City Press Limited
Letchworth, Hertfordshire SG6 1JS

Contents

Introduction   vii

Part I: Signs of Breakdown
Chapter 1:   Illiteracy   3
Chapter 2:   Violence and Indiscipline   11
Chapter 3:   Truancy   15
Chapter 4:   University Disorder   19
Chapter 5:   Collapse of Confidence   27
Chapter 6:   The Decline in General Culture and Personal Participation   33

Part II: The Reasons for Breakdown
Chapter 7:   Retreat from Authority   41
Chapter 8:   The Use of the Discovery Method   47
Chapter 9:   The Fashion for Change   55
Chapter 10:   The Comprehensive School   67
Chapter 11:   Destreaming—The New Frontier   83
Chapter 12:   The Egalitarian Millenarians   91
Chapter 13:   The Myth of Reverse Discrimination   97
Chapter 14:   The Attack on Examinations   107
Chapter 15:   The Fall in the Calibre of Teachers and Teacher Training   113
Chapter 16:   The Over-expansion of Universities   121
Chapter 17:   The Revolution That Never Was: The Visual and Electronic Cult   131

Part III: Plan for Revival
Chapter 18:   The Return of Authority   137
Chapter 19:   The Schools   141
Chapter 20:   Higher Education and Universities   153

Introduction

Wherever I go I am besieged by people, particularly parents, anxiously questioning the present state of British education. Are standards falling? Is discipline worse? Are children reading less well? What do you think of comprehensive schools? Is a university education worthwhile?

On my good days I am patient with my questioners. On my bad days I am abrupt or run for cover, but the questions go on. Was religion or salvation in the nineteenth century ever discussed to the extent that education is now, or was there such a variety of sects and prophets to choose from?

One does not need to be a follower of Ivan Illich or the Black Papers to realise that there is rising doubt about both the effectiveness and the values of much modern education. One only needs to talk to pupils, parents, employers and the general public. The December 1973 issue of *Social Trends* showed that while the majority of people recorded a high level of satisfaction with family life, housing and their job, satisfaction with their children's education was low.

How much is this scepticism justified and are there any remedies? In this volume I attempt to set out the objective evidence for concern. I also attempt to suggest what we, and others in Western Europe and America, must do to salvage our standards and to make our schools and universities more effective instruments in maintaining—or even restoring—a free, liberal and satisfying society. Inevitably, educational institutions will be judged by the values an individual cherishes, but we can at least agree on the need to test how far modern schooling attains its specified ends. Some of us will also question whether these ends are worthwhile.

PART I

Signs of Breakdown

Chapter 1

Illiteracy

The first of the three R's was and always will be reading. Just as deafness cuts a person off from his surroundings, so illiteracy cuts a person off from much knowledge of the past and many varied opinions of the present. His choice and ultimately freedom of thought is then circumscribed by what he hears from his friends and from popular performers on radio and television. The ability to sample, to reflect, to accept and to reject is gravely limited. I do not believe that the rolling wallpaper of television will ever replace the written word, and anyway the viewer must be able to read the programmes if he is to know what is being offered. The extreme sanctions used in Russia against an underground press and dissident authors demonstrate the continued power of reading to influence opinions, behaviour and the fortunes of the most mighty governments. Despite Somerset Maugham's tale of the church sexton, a person who cannot read is also severely limited in his private, personal and leisure life. In so many ways, a person who cannot read cannot fully enjoy the freedoms available to others in our society.

The first Protestant day and Sunday schools towards the end of the eighteenth century determined to make their scholars literate so that they could read their Bibles. From all accounts they proved highly efficient, and King James's Bible was hardly written in basic English. There was in the early nineteenth century a wide market in religious tracts and popular literature such as the penny magazines, serialised fiction, almanacs and ballads. Political views and news also became widely distributed and according to Samuel Bamford, the weaver-poet, William Cobbett's writings "were read on nearly every cottage hearth in the manufacturing district of

South Lancashire". Certainly Cobbett's *Address to the Journeymen and Labourers* sold 200,000 copies in two months.

The Reports of the Poor Law Commissioners, of the Factory Commissioners and surveys on the state of the hand loom weavers and on the state of education provide valuable information on the extent of adult literacy in the early nineteenth century. The standard of literacy then insisted upon was probably higher than the present test which is for a reading age of nine years, sufficient to read a popular newspaper. These reports showed that some 79 per cent of Northumberland and Durham miners could read in 1840 and that 92 per cent of adults in Hull were apparently literate in 1841. R. K. Webb estimates that between two-thirds and three-quarters of the working-class were literate in the 1830s, which was before the first government subventions to education in 1833 could have had effect.

Such high figures no longer surprise me since my historical research into the organisation of the Ashworth cotton mills near Bolton in the 1830s. The records brought to light a figure of 98 per cent literacy among the 561 mill operatives, as vouched by the factory inspectors and superintendents who certainly had no love for the Ashworths or their methods.*

R. K. Webb's estimate of literacy in the late 1870s correlates closely with the number of adults who had attended schools so that they would appear successful in attaining something like 100 per cent literacy among their students. The higher figures for the Ashworth mills arose because all their adults (in an early version of the "Open University") went to school in the evenings when they were recruited and the firm's policy was to encourage if not insist on literacy before promotion to more responsible and higher-paid work in the mills.

By the 1860s, before schooling became universal, it is very likely that nine-tenths of the rapidly increasing adult population were literate. Only Prussia had a higher percentage of her population in school attendance. In 1865 nearly 95 per cent of boys entering the Royal Navy and the Royal Marines could read, although most of them would be drawn from the lower strata of the working-class. W. E. Forster, when introducing the 1870 Education Act, like

* Rhodes Boyson: *The Ashworth Enterprise*, Oxford, 1970.

many who supported the Acts of 1876 and 1880, presumed that universal schooling would bring universal literacy. It never occurred to the optimistic Victorians that schooling up to the age of 11 could fail to make all children literate.

It is probable that at some point between 1880 and 1939 we came very near to this state of universal literacy. According to the late Professor Sir Cyril Burt, the distinguished psychologist and long-time adviser to the London County Council, the peak was reached around 1930. In 1931 a report of the Board of Education's Consultative Committee on the primary school disclosed that all but a few "backward" children could read by the age of seven. The acceptance of this report with little or no comment would seem to indicate how satisfactory standards then were.

Until the middle 1960s it was widely presumed that not only had we maintained standards but that smaller classes and the improved training of teachers had raised them still higher.

In 1966, however, a government-backed survey of the National Children's Bureau found that of 10,596 children aged seven some 37 per cent needed help in reading normally given to infants, while a further 10 per cent had barely begun to read. Since its conclusions were unfashionable this report sank almost without trace. Few if any were then ready to accept that standards had really declined.

The following year, 1967, saw the publication of the Plowden Report. Appendix 7 referred to "a remarkable improvement in standards of reading" since the Second World War and Table 1 showed the steady improvement in the reading of 11-year-old pupils between the years of 1948 and 1964. Few questioned these findings since in retrospect it seemed safe to assume that standards had improved since the war.

The year 1948 after all, was only three years after the end of a war which had seriously disrupted education in Britain and many of the children examined in that year had spent their early years in part-time schooling during the evacuation of London and other major cities. The fathers of the children aged 11 in 1948 had, with very many male teachers, been away in the armed services until 1945 or 1946, while fewer teachers had been trained for service in the schools. Thus with both school and home life seriously disturbed it was little wonder that standards were low in 1948 and had been considerably improved by 1964.

Two years later in 1969 Professor Burt published a table which showed that while standards of reading of London children had improved since 1945 they were still 6 per cent below the standard scores attained by 11-year-old children in 1930. He concluded, "Judged by tests applied and standardised in 1913–14, the average attainments in reading, spelling, mechanical and problem arithmetic are now appreciably lower than they were 55 years ago!"

While the peak score in reading comprehension was attained in 1930 the score of 1913–14 in spelling and problem arithmetic has not since been equalled. In the First World War the score in these two latter subjects fell away to recover to an almost equal level in 1920–30. The improvement after the Second World War, however, had not come to within 6 per cent of the 1914 figure in spelling nor to within 3 per cent of the 1914 figure in problem arithmetic, although both scores were still rising in 1965.

These figures of Professor Burt provoked great opposition and indignation in 1969 although there was already a rising ground-swell of parental and teacher opinion that there was something seriously wrong in the state of education and all was far from the best in the best of all possible worlds.

In 1971 it was alleged by the President of the National Association of Remedial Teachers that half of the adult illiterates were below the age of 25. Thus half the adult illiterates were drawn from the one-sixth of the adult population who had left school within the previous 10 years. Since literacy normally declines with lack of use in later life, it could have been assumed that less than one-sixth of the adult illiterates would have been drawn from these below the age of 25 if the schools had been of equal efficiency over the previous 50 or 60 years.

It was, however, the publication of the research of Dr. Brian Start and Mr. Kim Wells for the National Foundation for Educational Research which proved to be the watershed. *The Trend of Reading Standards* was published in the spring of 1972 and carefully analysed the results of tests of reading comprehension given to 7,150 pupils aged 11 and 15 in 300 state schools. It showed that the standards of 11-year-olds after being stagnant from 1960 had fallen since 1964. At the same time there had been no improvement in the standards of 15-year-olds since 1961. The very bright 11-year-olds were in 1971 three months behind the reading age of their 1964 equivalents, the least able 10 per cent were $3\frac{1}{2}$ months behind, and the middle group were six months behind their 1964 equivalents.

Some people queried the Start and Wells conclusions, pointing out that words used in the test since 1948 like "mannequin", "wheelwright", and "haberdasher" were little used or understood by children in 1971. "Haberdasher" certainly is obscure, while "wheelwright" may only come back with the decline of the motor-car, although Miss World and TV fashion shows on television may rescue "mannequin" sooner. Yet few had queried these words in 1964 when it was accepted that standards were rising. Furthermore, there were certain faults in the Start and Wells research which tended to overrate the 1971 score.

Not only were the large numbers of missing 15-year-olds absent from school and the tests in 1971 probably those most backward in reading, but schools which did not cooperate would tend to be those where reading standards were lowest. Nor could the low rate of only 73 per cent of the primary schools and 53 per cent of the secondary schools which returned the questionnaires be blamed entirely on the 1971 postal strike.

The verdict of Mrs. Vera Southgate of Manchester University, one of Britain's leading experts on literacy, was: "I accept this conclusion that there has been a drop in standards." Likewise Mrs. Thatcher, then Secretary of State at the Department of Education and Science, commented that "the main conclusions cannot be ignored".

T. R. Horton's *The Reading Standards in Wales*, published in 1973, again for the National Foundation for Educational Research, brought more news of falling standards. The proportion of 15-year-old illiterates and semi-illiterates in 1971 was in excess of the comparative figures for 1961. Because Wales has, for cultural and economic reasons, always laid great stress on literacy, numeracy and education, the figures of decline came as a sharp shock to many observers.

The situation in London gives even more cause for concern. A survey by the Inner London Education Authority completed in 1968 showed that eight-year-olds in London were six months behind children of similar age in other parts of the country in learning to read. When the same 32,000 children were surveyed in 1971 at the age of 11, they were as far behind the national average as they had been in 1968. The average reading age of the intake of some London comprehensive schools is two years behind their calendar age and a third of their intake has to be put into remedial and backward classes.

Today it is generally accepted that some 6 to 7 per cent of British school leavers are illiterate (having a reading age of below seven) and another 13–14 per cent are only semi-literate (having a reading age of below nine years which is generally accepted as the literary barrier).

Dr. Joyce Morris told a London conference on illiteracy in November 1973, that there were 3 million adults in Britain who, while not educationally subnormal, could not read the simplest of newspapers or understand the Highway Code. She also joined with Professor John Merritt, Professor of Education at the Open University, in attacking the "dangerous and pernicious nonsense" preached by the Canadian English professor, Marshall McLuhan, and his followers that books and their reading were obsolete.

At the same conference a poignant description by Mr. Geoffrey Clarkson, a former prison chaplain in Liverpool, brought home the horror and isolation of illiteracy. He described the illiterate driver's mate who refused promotion because he hated to admit that he could not read and feared having to face the bizarre images of road signs, maps, log books, time-sheets and delivery notes. Taking refuge in a lower job with absolutely no prospects, the man admitted that "the empty spectacle case in his top pocket, the array of cheap ballpoints he carried, and the bandage on his hand were all ploys to hide his illiteracy".

Following *The Trend of Reading Standards*, Mrs. Thatcher set up the Bullock Committee on literacy and oracy which reported in 1975. The Bullock Report is in some ways an amazing document. It first stated that the position regarding falling standards of literacy was not serious and then attempted to outline what should be done to rectify *falling* standards of literacy.

The Inquiry, like a Chinese Maoist comment where we must read in what we can, noted, "There seems to be a case for saying children of seven are not as advanced as formerly in those aspects of reading ability which are measured by tests". Presumably this means in plain English that standards had declined.

This decline is blamed not on modern methods but because these methods have been misunderstood. The Inquiry had "talked to young teachers who have so misunderstood them [modern methods] as to believe they should never directly teach the children". This means both that Colleges of Education train teachers inefficiently and that teachers should teach directly at least in some lessons.

The Inquiry also considered that Colleges of Education had placed too much emphasis on "psychology, sociology and child development" rather than the training of techniques for teaching reading. It also suggested that there should be more attention to spelling and even handwriting and it has much to say in defence of examinations.

The Note of Dissent from Mr. Stuart Froome to this Inquiry recognised the true position. He was an ex-headteacher who blamed the decline in literacy on reading readiness, the stress on creativity instead of discipline, and the discovery method.

Christopher Jencks, of the Center for Educational Policy Research at Harvard University, in his book *Inequality* describes poverty as the inability to participate in a social system. If almost all homes have telephones, those without suffer "poverty" in this sense. Similarly, if the withdrawal of public transport prevents a person without a car from meeting his friends, he is also in poverty. If lack of television prevents a person from discussing the serials and shows he may be said to suffer an element of poverty. On this definition the inability to read the newspapers certainly cuts a person off from political, social, sports and gambling news and even from comic strips, and is a form of poverty. For "illiteracy" read isolation and mental stunting.

These figures of illiteracy quoted earlier are not just a British problem. Professor Jacques Barzun has said that there are 25 million "functional illiterates" in the USA who cannot live fully because of insufficient reading and writing skills. The National

Reading Center in the United States announced in 1973 that more than 20 per cent of Americans over the age of 16 could not understand at least 10 per cent of standard application forms for such things as drivers' licences, bank loans and job applications.

There are thus three crises in literacy: standards are static or falling; many bright children are functioning below their mental age; and there is an increasing segment of our population unable to cope with everyday life because of illiteracy.

There is also a subsidiary crisis in the economic use of human and material resources. The adult illiterate and under-functioning semi-illiterate have been produced by an educational system which now keeps pupils at school until the age of 16, compared with the 10- or 11-year-old leavers of 1870. The pupil-teacher ratio has been reduced from 120 pupils for each teacher (assisted by three monitors) in 1870 to 22 pupils to a teacher now, and there have also been massive increases in the expenditure on books and visual aids. If adult literacy in 1970 is lower than in 1914 or even 1870 then one must question whether education is making good use of its rising share of national resources. This question should not be resented by the educational establishment because without basic literacy, numeracy and the teaching of the skills of learning no cultural superstructure can be built.

Chapter 2

Violence and Indiscipline

It is important to be as analytical and unemotional about violence and truancy in schools as it is to approach objectively the figures for illiteracy. The odd horror story of violence makes the headlines but what matters is the national picture and how it compares with the situation 10, 20 or 50 years ago, however difficult it is to quantify the comparison.

The assessment of the present position is also handicapped by the conspiracy of silence which naturally tends to surround the figures for violence and truancy in many schools and authorities. No one wishes to show his worst aspect to the world and teachers and educational administrators are no exception to this general rule. There is also a suspicion that heads and teachers who draw attention to their difficulties may be overlooked in the promotion stakes and that an education officer's hopes of a peaceful relationship with his committee and his eventual award of honours is put at risk if he brings unpleasant facts to public light.

In this situation the National Association of Schoolmasters (NAS)—that organ of militant but hardheaded male teachers now tenuously linked with the Union of Women Teachers—has performed a public service by drawing attention to the problems of violence in schools. It has claimed that 2,000 British teachers were attacked in 1971 and listed cases of vicious assaults on women teachers, pupils who kicked teachers in the groin or face, pupils who had tried to set fire to classrooms during lessons, and a number of school knifings.

Dr. Lowenstein, educational psychologist in Hampshire, prepared, in 1972, a report for the NAS which counted 5,994 recent cases of violence in secondary schools and 783 in primary schools, in addition to 3,200 cases of *uncontrollable* pupil violence in 415 schools. Dr. Bilsen's research in 1973 also showed that at least one in ten boys surveyed in London were either attracted to violence or were enthusiastic about it.

Specific publicised local instances of violence, protection rackets and bullying can be added to these national figures. Sir Alec Clegg, Chief Education Officer of the West Riding of Yorkshire, referred to a decline in school standards with an increase in violence, vandalism, crime and child difficulties. Leeds Education Committee, after considering a report which listed 60 attacks on teachers and more than 300 children having to be parted from their classmates because of aggression, considered the formation of a "crash" five-man team of teachers who could be rushed to troubled schools in that city. In November 1973, 30 teachers in Ellesmere Port blacklisted five pupils they were determined not to teach and wanted banned for attacking other pupils and threatening and shouting obscenities at teachers so that normal discipline with ordinary pupils was at the point of breakdown.

One Luton headmaster resigned his headship in 1974 following parental allegations of bullying, vandalism and shoplifting under his liberal regime and every child in his 1,250-pupil school walked out in support of demands to bring back the cane. The number of pupils suspended in Glasgow more than doubled between 1967–8 and 1972–3 and increased five-fold in Renfrewshire between 1965–6 and 1972–3. High Wycombe Schoolmasters' Association asked the local education authority in 1973 to protect teachers against classroom violence.

There are schools in London and beyond where pupils have so terrorised the local shopkeepers and their customers that these shops are closed completely or banned to pupils during the lunch break. Cases of children setting fire to schools have recently doubled every four years and are likely to reach 1,000 a year by 1980. In 1973 fires causing individual damage of over £10,000 occurred in 89 schools and cost a total of £5,600,000. One Islington nursery school in that year was fired by six-year-olds who also battered to death the guinea pigs, mutilated the fish and used a caged bird as a football.

In 1973–4 cases of school blackmail and protection rackets were listed in the press in areas as far apart as London, Bridgend, Glamorgan, and Malling in Kent. One boy in Sutton took a knife to school in self-defence and killed the bully who attacked him and there were numerous cases, as at Luton and Faversham, of parents keeping their children at home because they feared the school bullies. Luton sent one girl away to private school at the ratepayers' expense after she had stayed away from a comprehensive school for seven months because she alleged she was punched and kicked by other girls. Where 25 years ago it was the badly-behaved boy who played truant, it may now be the good boy who stays at home for his own protection. There was also in 1973 at least one murder which the parents blamed on the terrorisation of their girl by school bullies.

Adolescent violence has increased ten-fold in 20 years and it would be both difficult and naive to absolve the schools of all responsibility. Schools reflect the values of society but they also help to create them. It is difficult to believe that the potential behaviour patterns of pupils have changed greatly in the last 20 years. It is possible that it is both the sense of authority within schools and the enforcement of school rules which have changed or weakened. It is certain that if pupils cannot be compelled to observe reasonable rules and a fair code of behaviour within schools, they will certainly not obey them when they leave school.

It is possible that it is not the figures for violence and arson which are the greatest threat to schools but the lesson resisters of the classroom. A teacher can be undermined as efficiently by dumb insolence, time wasting and non-cooperation of pupils as by physical threats or obscene insults, although the former may lead to the latter. Persistent chattering, a disinclination to study and deliberate failure to bring pens, paper and books to a lesson can easily escalate to insolence and open rebellion. It is the strain on city teachers of the battle for class control, particularly in secondary schools, which saps their confidence and optimism and drives many of them out of teaching.

The situation in parts of the USA is even more alarming than in Britain. Arson in schools in Miami, Florida cost £384,000 in 1971. At Sacramento, California, portable ultrasonic alarms in the shape of a fountain pen have been tested so that teachers can call for help when pupils riot.

The New York Board of Education in 1972 spent £2,500,000 in employing an extra 1,200 guards to protect teachers in its 900 schools. More than half of New York's 70 high schools have policemen attached to protect both the teachers and property from students and infiltrators. Teachers there have called for "combat money" because of the increase in rapes and robberies in the classrooms. In the first nine months of 1972 there were in New York schools 4 murders, 496 robberies, 326 burglaries and 28 rapes while in the first five months of 1973 a different definition of offences produced 2,200 serious assaults on teachers and students and at least 825 robberies, many of them armed. One New York school has 19 aides and seven karate-trained guards to watch its 20 entrances.

There is also in New York a phenomenon which is becoming more familiar in the United Kingdom—the risk to order created by invasion from outside by gangs, sometimes from other schools. School robberies have increased in Britain, as in America, as more expensive electronic equipment is placed in schools. The morale of housemasters in Highbury Grove was certainly not helped when their studies were gone over by outside burglars three times in three months. An even greater menace which has happened in South London, is of outside or other schools' marauders coming through a school looking for victims or to seek a battle-ground.

Even in Sweden there is a lack of discipline, particularly in urban schools. There, too, teachers are beset with disobedience, bordering on violence. A government commission was set up in 1972 to study absenteeism, drug addiction and drunkenness in Swedish schools.

One doesn't expect all children to sit for ever in orderly rows moving by numbers and holding their pens ever at the ready, but a certain order is necessary to allow for teaching. The London University Institute of Education, in its evidence to the James Committee on Teacher Training, stated "there are schools where conditions are such that no teacher, let alone a young and new teacher, can be expected to teach". That grim evidence should serve as a warning to British educationalists.

Chapter 3

Truancy

Compulsory state schooling which was first stipulated in the 1880 Education Act can be upheld as efficient only if in practice it enforces the attendance of all pupils of compulsory school age, which in Britain is now from 5 to 16, having been raised from the age of 15 in September 1973. The minimum school-leaving age is actually higher than 16 since pupils can only leave at the end of the spring and summer terms. Thus a pupil who became 16 on the 3rd September 1973 was unable to leave until the 9th April 1974, when he or she would be 16 years 7 months.

As with violence, it is very difficult to obtain comparative figures of school attendance over a period of years. Accordingly, we have to rely on indications gleaned from speeches, reports and researches.

The secretary of the National Association of Chief Welfare Officers said in 1973 that some 5 per cent of school children—500,000 in number—played truant every week before the raising of the school-leaving age. The president of the same Association is on record as estimating that in early 1973 420,000 children were absent from school on any average day without good reason.

I suspect that these figures are an underestimate, even if the definition of truancy is taken as those who were not marked on school registers and provided no reasonable excuse to explain their absence. Pupil absences have at times risen to 20 per cent in Salford, 12 per cent in Manchester, Devon and London, 10 per cent in Liverpool and to 33 per cent in Merton secondary schools. If one allows that 5 per cent of pupils are sick or have other genuine reasons for absence, then a national attendance of 89–90 per cent will mean that well over 500,000 pupils are daily playing truant from our schools.

Such a 5–7 per cent national truancy rate means that the average pupil misses up to two terms of his total schooling through truancy. This according to the speech of Edwin Noble to the National Union of Teachers (NUT) Annual Educational Conference in December 1972 is itself an underestimate. He claimed that not only were one in four Manchester schoolchildren absent some time in each week but that the average Manchester schoolchild lost a full year of his period of compulsory school attendance through absence.

All these figures date from before the latest raising of the school leaving age and it has been estimated that truancy in many secondary schools increased by up to 50 per cent after this event. Indeed, since an earlier report on the Inner London Education Authority (ILEA) showed that approximately twice as many 15-year-olds as 11-year-olds absented themselves from schools, a large increase of truancy following the raising of the school-leaving age was to be expected. The Department of Education and Science survey of truancy made on the 17th January 1974, and published in July of that year was based upon arrangements that hid this increase of truancy—schools were warned of the day of check and each school defined which absentees were truants.

There are schools where attendance has dropped to below 75 per cent, or even to below 50 per cent over a month or a term. One London comprehensive school has a published attendance figure of 67 per cent for a full year. Mr. Harvey Hinds, chairman of the schools committee of ILEA, confessed in April 1974 that two out of five fifth-year children were truanting from some London schools.

Figures of attendance already quoted refer to those marked present on the register. The August 1973 issue of *Where* threw serious doubt on the reliability of such figures and it is becoming more widely recognised that all pupils who register at 9 am may not still be in school at 10 am or even 9.30 am. Huge new city comprehensive schools with low railings and numerous gates, ineffectiveness of many teachers in keeping discipline, continuous lesson changes and walks of up to ten minutes between classes encourage casual truancy with boys and girls slipping in and out of school.

The non-enforcement of "compulsory" school attendance has a number of serious consequences: it brings the law into disrepute and children obviously show that they have little respect for the schools they play truant from or the education they are escaping. Many truants, as the police point out, drift into delinquency. The Chief Constable of Birmingham has blamed the increased number of children playing truant from school for the sharp rise in shoplifting by juveniles in that city during school hours. In Glasgow in 1973 more than 2,600 of those arrested for shoplifting were under 16. About one-third were playing truant at the time. At Southwark in 1974 truant schoolchildren were involved in car crimes and daylight burglaries.

High figures for truants could mean that a new sub-criminal class, worthy of the pen of Charles Dickens, was being produced. A boy who first slipped casually out of school with impunity may begin to frequent the sleazier cafés with his friends until he is encouraged to turn to shoplifting and petty crime. It is a very unhealthy state of affairs.

There is evidence that certain countries are beginning to question the usefulness of a protracted period of compulsory school attendance. New Zealand, which had a school leaving age of 15, altered her laws in 1973 so that a boy or girl could leave at any age with the agreement of parents, teachers and school guidance advisers. France, where the minimum school-leaving age was raised to 16 in 1967, allows children to go to a Collège Technique or into apprenticeship at the age of 14. China has also reduced the normal length of her compulsory school attendance, where it is enforced, to nine or ten years. Italy has a school leaving age of 14 and Holland of $14\frac{1}{2}$. In Italy it is even estimated that 25–30 per cent of pupils cease to attend school before they are 13 years old.

Disillusion with the effects of a 16+ minimum school-leaving age in Britain has already communicated itself to leading educationalists and politicians. Dr. Harry Judge, Director of the Oxford University Department of Education, has called the raising of the school-leaving age "a mindless error". The National Association of Head Teachers voted for its reduction at their 1974 conference. Clement Freud, MP, Liberal Party spokesman on education, moved a motion in Parliament in 1974 to reduce the school-leaving age, Mr. Nigel Lawson, MP, did the same from the Conservative benches and Mr. Norman St. John Stevas, MP, Conservative Shadow Minister of Education, spoke in July 1974 in favour of a more flexible leaving date and for permission for boys to leave for apprenticeships and to the services at the age of 15.

Chapter 4

University Disorder

Sir Eric Ashby has defined the function of universities as "preserving, transmitting and enriching culture". They are institutions where scholars can meet to teach, to discuss, to research and to learn. Their mission is to seek by all rational means for truth which can be found only in a setting of free discussion and enquiry. When such an atmosphere is destroyed there are no true universities. They certainly cannot continue to exist alongside arbitrary or dogmatic beliefs or where physical force or intimidation has replaced open debate in reaching conclusions. They are not political or religious institutions with a commitment to change —any more than to preserve unchanged—the social, economic or political nature of a society.

There have recently been a number of signs that British universities are in danger of losing sight of their real purpose: the intimidation of visiting speakers whose views are unpopular with extremist left-wing opinion, the refusal of university authorities to provide platforms for such speakers, the attempt by students to change university policy by the use of force, the pressure to organise universities on one huge committee system ruled by majority vote, and the development of a large student union organisation with overt political aims.

One weapon of the extreme left and other vociferous minorities has been to raise so many protests and threats against an invited guest speaker that to preserve university order (and slowly strangle freedom of expression) the university authorities have refused to provide a room for a meeting. As early as 1968 a Conservative students' meeting at Lancaster University was prohibited by the Vice-Chancellor because opposing students had threatened to invade and disrupt it.

By 1970 right-wing Conservative MPs, like Patrick Wall and Ronald Bell, could speak at universities only at the risk of sloganised abuse of an unpleasant and intimidating nature. Mr. Duong Hong Duc, the Second Secretary of the Vietnamese Embassy, was forced to leave a Liberal Society meeting of the London School of Economics when members of the Socialist Society intimidated him and his suit was scorched by a firework. Even Joan Lestor, MP, Parliamentary Under-Secretary at the Department of Education and Science in the then Labour Government, had to rebuke hecklers at the National Union of Students' (NUS) Conference in April 1970, for threatening to destroy the right of free speech.

By 1970 groups of university students were not limiting their activities to opposing visiting lecturers. They were demanding more and more say in the organisation of universities with the intention of taking them over for their own political purposes. The year 1969 had seen the troubles at Essex which specifically began as a "liberal" university that would treat its staff and students equally in all respects. There were to be no petty rules or regulations but the provision of mixed accommodation and even common staff–student accommodation. It was a product, like the open plan school, of the idea of no boundaries, no structure and no hierarchy.

The discovery by Warwick University students of confidential files on students during their break-in to the university administrative area was used to inflame students against dons as their natural enemies. This was linked at Warwick with allegations about the improper pressures of big business on university autonomy. As students learned such tactical "grievances" from American campuses, Kent and East Anglia and other universities suffered similar student break-ins, and "confidential files" became a great war cry.

The ostensible objection of the students was to references to student political attitudes in confidential files but many unexceptionable and harmless grievances were exploited as an excuse to sharpen confrontations between aggrieved students and the university authorities. The civilised relationship of scholar and student was deliberately undermined so that the very essence of a scholarly university community was threatened. The mutual confidence on which teaching and learning are based was being systematically destroyed as student agitators searched diligently for further grievances. The game was given away by the slogan outside one university which said "Give us our demands today, we shall have new ones tomorrow".

The extreme student Left was already aiming to change universities from centres of free discussion and learning to centres of perpetual mass meetings of hundreds and thousands of students attending Maoist-style talk-ins which aimed to raise the "political consciousness" of the student. Where they could not control an elected student Council or Executive they used the intimidation and exhaustion of the mass meeting.

The Times in a first leading article on the 12th May, 1970 thus described the scene:

The extreme student left is at its worst one of the nastiest political phenomena that Britain has experienced in this century. Their contempt for discussion, their arrogance, their bile, and their willingness to resort to violence are reminiscent of the youth movements of totalitarian parties. They sometimes support causes deserving of sympathy but that seems often to be merely for tactical motives. For them the point of any cause is not its merit but the contribution it can make to their agitation.

Although matters quietened down after 1970 the peace was uneasy and the confidence of many university dons had been shattered by earlier events. The year 1973, however, saw three very unpleasant university scenes: a drunken demonstration at Stirling University during the visit of the Queen and the death of the Vice-Chancellor there from a heart attack at the time of the disturbances; the prevention by physical violence of Professor Eysenck's address at the London School of Economics; and the disruption of a lecture by Professor Huntingdon of Harvard at Sussex University.

Professor Eysenck was assaulted and thrown off the platform

by a student group of the Communist Party of England (Marxist-Leninist) from Birmingham and although their names were collected no action was taken. That Professor Eysenck's speech on current theories of intelligence was later published and proved uncontroversial did not set matters right. The occasion had been another victory for dogmatic student censorship.

The Sussex University authorities learned that a crowd of left-wing anti-American students would disrupt the lecture by Professor Huntingdon on "The Role of the Military in US Foreign Policy" for no better reason than that he was accused of some official link with American Air Force policy against the North Vietnamese. This was parallel with the objection by Essex University students to a lecture by a scholar who was alleged to have done research on germ warfare. No effective action was taken by the Sussex authorities before or after the disruption of Professor Huntington and a number of Sussex university academics actually supported the action of the students.

November 1973 also saw the withdrawal of an invitation for Mr. Enoch Powell, MP, to speak at Durham University when the Registrar told the Union Society, which had invited Mr. Powell, that none of the university buildings in the student residential areas could be used for fear of the threat of thuggery. Proof of the drift away from belief in freedom of speech was that the withdrawal of this invitation passed with hardly a mention in the British press.

This problem of how universities are to guarantee freedom of speech to visiting lecturers opposed by a militant section of students is far from easy to solve. If order cannot be guaranteed, it is probable that universities will have to expel students who demand freedom to express their own ideas whilst claiming the right to censor free expression by other students or lecturers. Without acceptance of the principle of the reciprocity of freedom, it is probable that universities as we have known them will cease to exist.

In April 1974 the NUS drew up a blacklist of speakers that students would, if necessary by force, prevent addressing student audiences. Speakers were prevented from addressing audiences at the Central London Polytechnic, Hatfield Polytechnic and

Newcastle University. Two months later the NUS apparently abandoned its policy of breaking up meetings. Such gatherings were, however, to be prevented by denying funds to any university society which invited "extreme" right-wing speakers. The action of members of the Labour Government in refusing to speak at universities until the original ban was withdrawn was as commendable as the support given to the ban by certain academics was deplorable.

There was also in 1973 and 1974 a number of student sit-ins or take-overs. Ostensibly aimed at reducing catering or residential charges or increasing student grants, they were used by the militant left to serve their own purposes. Turmoil once again engulfed Essex where the university offices were broken into and selected comments on staff and students from the files were read over the university radio station presumably under Pierre-Joseph Proudhon's slogan "property [including files] is theft". The applications for entry of 900 students were held up and thousands of pounds worth of property damaged. The Vice-Chancellor of Essex was harassed by the same methods which were used against the Vice-Chancellor of Stirling University; post-midnight telephone calls, raids on his house, a brick through his window and threatening letters to his wife and his family.

At the North London Polytechnic there seemed to be a continued attempt by a minority of students owing allegiance to the hardline International Socialists (a Trotskyist group) to take over full control. The Student Union President was in his sixth year at the Polytechnic, three as a full-time NUS official paid from the public purse. The Director's office was ransacked and confidential letters circulated. The sit-in there ended only when clerical and technical union members, weary of the whole business, gave notice of the withdrawal of their labour.

At Reading University in 1973 police had to rescue Professor Henry Pitt, the Vice-Chancellor, from a chanting mob of 200 students, and at Oxford the International Marxists and International Socialists with their supporters occupied the Examination Schools. The use of police at Reading University is interesting because most university agitators claim to be under no law apart from revolutionary law and explicitly refuse to accept the authority of the university proctors as a feudal vestige while they claim the police have no authority on the campus. For their part university authorities are reluctant to call in the police since this could break up further the sense of university community.

Essex in 1973 provided an illustration of a university where the militant left did not have full control of the students' elected Council so they ruled by mass meetings like a revolutionary commune with no genuine student debate. Groups of extremist students were ferried round the country like gangs of flying pickets to stir up trouble while Essex in turn was visited by students from Leeds, Hull, Southampton, East Anglia and other universities arriving in buses hired at public expense.

Since some student union officers are elected by polls as low as 3 per cent, it is generally not difficult for militant students to gain control of their unions and be elected to the full-time posts. Most students ignore union activities and concentrate on their studies and their personal interests. In this way the militant left has full-time agitators available armed with funds compulsorily levied on the majority. There are six full-time student officers at the North London Polytechnic. Funds can be given to organisations like the Black Panthers, striking workers, Sinn Fein, Bangla Desh, the Viet Cong and the militant African movements while, as at York and Southampton, reputable Conservative groups of students are denied all help. Essex University received an inscribed plaque from Long Kesh thanking members for their support.

All students are compulsorily conscripted into their local students' union and in almost all cases these are affiliated to the National Union of Students which has 610,000 nominal members and the use of considerable monies. Nationally it is controlled by a broad alliance made up largely of members of the Communist Party, a few members of the Labour Party, some non-aligned Socialists and assorted protesters. The opposition at its Conferences is provided by the International Socialists and the International Marxists. In reality a minority of a minority, the NUS takes part in all national discussions on students and is treated as part of a ruling establishment.

The NUS extreme left-wing leadership sees the student–don confrontation as part of a revolutionary uprising to overthrow liberal capitalism. It is noticeable that when there was an inquiry at Essex university in 1974 the Student President asked for this to be made by someone who was familiar with trade union disputes and not a senior academic. When the NUS launched its campaign in November 1973 for bigger student grants it claimed that this was part of the "working-class struggle against the capitalist system".

It is as well to remember that disorder was only prevented at certain universities by capitulation to every student demand. At York University, after a boycott and a sit-in by students who demanded the abolition of the Part 1 examination as a section of the social science degree course, all 177 candidates were allowed to take their papers at home. In 38 cases plagiarism and collusion were proved. These students were, however, allowed to continue their course and to resit the examination in March 1974, with the understanding that only those who passed could continue their course. Five failed but under student protest they were again allowed to continue their course. Meanwhile the University had decided to abolish the Part 1 examination and replace it, as the students wished, by continuous assessment. It was little wonder that the whole of the economics teaching faculty in the university, fearful for the standing of the York degree, dissociated itself from these events by public disclaimer.

There was similar capitulation at Kent University in February 1974, when the university senate gave in to student demands and the occupation of the administrative offices and reinstated a student who had failed his examinations. Two dons resigned following this appeasement.

Intimidation and open violence have also occurred at many European universities. In Holland the occupation of university buildings and the disruption of lectures continue to be the two standard tactics of student rebels but the extremists are also trying to use student representation on the newly-created academic councils to "politicise" both the academic curriculum and the appointment of staff.

The same has happened in West Germany where the politicians have insisted upon students and non-academic staff being represented on university governing bodies. In January 1974 when a

Christian Democrat Professor of Economics was appointed at Frankfurt University, there was a massive boycott of lectures led by the Communist Student League. The process of "politicisation", the spread of Marxist ideas, has gone further in West Berlin, Bremen, Hamburg and some other West German universities. In 1973 at Sussex University the students had a large say in the appointment of a new lecturer for the history and social studies course.

In Denmark where there is 50 per cent student representation on appointing committees, almost every official university course is also shadowed by a "parallel counter-course" organised by "radicals" and designed to draw students away from the official courses. Such pervasive and persistent political interference can extinguish academic freedom as effectively as in Communist or Fascist states.

Some American universities have to recruit both staff and students, as at the University of Illinois, under special "minority group" clauses irrespective of the academic merit of the applicants. There is also pressure in America to put restrictions on social science and other research likely to "jeopardise the reputation or status of individual and social groups". The obscurantist opponents of Galileo are still with us now in the guise of extremist student "radicals" who are invariably backward-looking revolutionaries. They are encouraged by weak or well-intentioned governments.

The price of liberty in universities, as in life as a whole, is eternal vigilance. The opposition to free speech and free inquiry, and the demand for "concerned" or "committeed" universities promoting "relevant" social, political and economic action rather than learning or research, threaten this freedom. The plea for egalitarianism and mass participation does not help. The cry that "Jack is as good as his master"—that the most callow undergraduate's view is as important as that of the most learned professor—can do a university untold harm. Unless this danger is taken more seriously, many of our 250,000 university students could find themselves attending indoctrinating sessions instead of learned lectures and this could have dire consequences for the future of a free society.

Chapter 5

Collapse of Confidence

A healthy school system must win the allegiance of teachers, parents and the public. Among all three there is unmistakable evidence of a sharp fall in confidence.

The lack of confidence of teachers is shown by the numbers of qualified practitioners who leave the profession, the rapid turnover of staff in many parts of the country, the low qualifications of those entering the profession, and the increasing militancy of teachers who, like university students, adopt an "us versus them" posture in dealing with senior colleagues or the authorities.

The wastage-rate of teachers in the early years of teaching is very high. After a three-year College of Education course costing the country some £3,000, four-fifths of the women and one-third of the men leave the profession within their first six years of teaching. Even among the number of women teachers who leave for childbirth, it is doubtful how many will return to education except under economic necessity.

There are two elements in the problem of teacher turnover. The first is the rapid turnover from school to school in the search for higher pay through special responsibility allowances, and the second is the flight of teachers from many urban authorities because of the pressure of living costs and the increasing difficulty in maintaining discipline. Both factors are ultimately influential in causing so many teachers to leave the profession. The flight of teachers from London and other cities is, however, a new phenomenon which is matched by the difficulty of staffing other public services in urban areas.

A survey by the Assistant Masters Association (AMA) in 1973, showed that between a quarter and a fifth of London teachers from both ILEA and the outer London boroughs, left each year.

The highest figure was 29·8 per cent in Brent and the lowest was 17·3 per cent in Hillingdon. This disturbed and disturbing state of affairs cannot simply be blamed on low salaries which themselves reflect over a number of years the low esteem in which teachers are held by the rest of society.

There has always been a conflict in the minds of teachers as to whether they are a profession or a trade. Supporters of the view that teaching is a profession have aimed to create for themselves a highly responsible, highly respected image, believing that society would then be prepared to pay teachers high salaries. Those who saw teaching as a trade wished to ape the militant trade unionists, to negotiate vigorously and even belligerently with the employers and to strike if the terms offered were unsatisfactory.

The National Union of Schoolmasters, basically a union of career male teachers, has always been militant but well-controlled in the tradition of the old trade unions, taking action only with the approval or guidance of its national headquarters. It has organised courses for shop stewards in the schools and occasionally calls strikes in favour of higher wages or better conditions of service in some school or authority.

The National Union of Teachers, a large union whose strength lies in its primary school membership, has moved towards militancy, partially in defence of the living standards of its members and partially under the influence of Neo-Troskyist and rank-and-file groups which have taken over some branches that can only be kept as members if they are given their head. Like the militant university students, these branches look for confrontation with their employers not only to improve the conditions of service of their members but also to express political opposition to certain policies.

The end of teaching as a profession was signalled by the determination of the NUT in London from 1973–4 to cease to "cover" for absent colleagues after three days, far more than by the NUT (or the NAS) joining in membership of the Trades Union Congress, a decision taken by the NUT Executive only after the proposal had been rejected by a ballot of members. The Joint Four teacher unions, the National Association of Head Teachers and the Professional Association of Teachers continue to make an attempt to keep the image of professionalism alive.

The growing disillusion of parents with the state educational system is shown in three ways: their refusal to send their children to certain schools to which the local education authorities have directed them, their objection to the teaching methods and values of certain schools which their children are attending, and the increased numbers sending their children to independent schools.

The ILEA has borne the brunt of parental protests against the way children are allocated to secondary schools. In 1972, of 33,000 primary pupils due for transfer to secondary schools, some 4,645 did not get the school of their first choice. Over 2,500 parents protested to the divisional officers but something like half of the parents accepted the schools they were then offered for their children.

Large groups of parents, however, continued to object to the schools they were offered. Their chief reasons were not that the schools were in old buildings or had a low teacher/pupil ratio, but that they objected to the low academic standards, the lax discipline and even the loose curriculum of these schools. Some 800 children were still out of school at the beginning of the September term, 1972, 560 remained out towards the end of September and 325 had not attended school by late October.

The protesting parents in Islington and Hackney, who were predominantly working-class, joined together to rent a hall and hire three teachers for their children. They continued to give the ILEA a worrying time: police had to clear demonstrators from at least one divisional office, parents chained themselves to the railings at County Hall and held a school in the main foyer. Mr. Harvey Hinds, the chairman of the ILEA schools committee, was held hostage in a Stoke Newington school until police intervention secured his release.

It is significant that none of the parents who kept their children away from ILEA schools was prosecuted for the non-attendance of their sons and daughters and that almost all of them finished up obtaining either the school they wanted or an equally respected school for their children. It was February 1973 before the last of the "rebellious" pupils entered a school of their choice.

Although the ILEA was more careful in its allocation of pupils in 1973, a smaller number of parents again kept their children from the schools offered and once more a school was opened in Islington and a teacher hired until the ILEA fed the pupils into the preferred schools as soon as the numbers were manageable.

Towards the end of 1973 there was also an increase in the number of Moslem immigrant parents who kept their girls out of school because they objected to mixed schools. Although this objection was based on social and religious rather than educational grounds, it illustrates discontent with the narrow choice provided by the local education authorities.

Leicestershire has seen at least two revolts against comprehensive secondary schools to whose methods and values many parents strongly objected. Parents of some 250 children at Countesthorpe College petitioned the Department of Education and Science for the right of parents to choose an education they considered best for their children. According to the local press, this petition was prepared because the parents considered the school was far too left-wing, progressive and permissive. The question of an inquiry into the organisation of this school became an issue in the county elections in April 1973 and it was finally agreed that a Department of Education and Science (DES) inquiry into the school should be held.

Some hundred parents also objected to the lack of discipline, poor academic standards and lack of a competitive element at Wreake Valley Comprehensive College, Leicestershire, and a working party of governors, staff and parents was set up after the parents met the Board of Governors and the Principal in June 1973.

The objection of parents to particular schools is a sign of a breakdown of minimum standards in the state system during the past 20 years. Before that period there were "identikit" grammar schools and secondary modern schools with dependable standards. Today there is no standard comprehensive school and parents often object to the school place their children are allocated in the bingo lottery of the state system. There is no longer a dependable general pattern of internal school organisation or even in the general approach to the education of the young.

It is no doubt these growing discrepancies between state schools and the fear of parents that their children may be allocated to what are called "sink" schools which help to account for the increased number of children entering independent education. Compared with 564 pupils in the ILEA who left the state sector at the time of transfer to secondary school at the age of 11 in 1971, the number had increased to 735 a year later.

Certainly the demand for independent education is increasing. The number of pupils in Headmasters' Conference schools increased from 84,700 in 1947 to 105,000 in 1967, while the number in direct grant schools rose from 62,000 to 78,000. The largest increase, however, has recently come in the preparatory schools taking pupils from 7–9 to 13 years. Despite the pressures of inflation on family expenditure, the total number of children attending these schools increased by 1,477 in 1972 and by a further 4,000 in 1973 to a total of 70,000. This is as much a vote of no confidence in the state educational system as it is a vote of confidence in the independent sector.

Recently, we have seen a marginal increase in Britain of interest in both "free schools" and "deschooling". Free schools, with less discipline and an attempt at self-rule by pupils, are not new and support for them has risen and fallen over the last two hundred years. Despite the fame of A. S. Neill, however, "free schools" are not a significant factor in the British educational system. Support for them outside certain middle-class intellectual families is small or non-existent and the total numbers attending such schools in Britain are less than the number enrolled in one average-sized secondary modern school.

It is the same segment of the intellectual middle-class, influenced by a romantic primitive view of life and Ivan Illich in America, which also toys with the idea of "deschooling". It is argued that structured education fulfils no useful purpose for pupils and lessens their own individuality and spontaneity whilst shaping them as tools for some authoritarian or conventional society. On this reckoning, schools should be closed and pupils should get their education from the real world. Its simplicity makes this an attractive if facile doctrine and its appeal to the social worker mentality should alert us to the danger of its influence spreading. That anyone takes "deschooling" seriously in an urban industrialised society, however, shows how deep is the crisis of confidence in state education.

There is clearly enough evidence of widespread lack of confidence to prompt the question: Do these accumulating signs of breakdown in schools and universities spring from a common underlying cause?

Chapter 6

The Decline in General Culture and Personal Participation

When the supporters of the new educational theories are confronted with such facts as the decline in literacy, the increase in school violence, truancy and the rise of irresponsible behaviour in the universities, their defence is that the last hundred years has seen an increase in human happiness and standards of general culture and that these increases are due to educational achievements.

There are no really satisfactory methods of testing comparative human happiness but certain comparisons can be made between cultural standards and the degree of individual participation in 1870 with those of the present time.

A century ago, there was very little higher education. Only a handful of clergymen and doctors had university degrees. Yet a study of any local newspaper in Lancashire or Yorkshire in the 1870s would provide a surprisingly high tone of serious and informed discussion in the news, leader and correspondence columns. There was generally as much coverage of Parliamentary news in a weekly or bi-weekly local town newspaper as is now given daily in *The Times*. This says a great deal for both the status of Parliament and the political maturity, knowledge and curiosity of the general population.

There was certainly a great interest in national politics. In 1868 in Haslingden, an East Lancashire cotton town with a population of some 12,000, there was a Liberal procession of 4,000 people accompanied by 12 bands and 50 horsemen apart from the carriages of gentry. After a tea attended by 2,000 people, there were evening meetings in various halls. Since only 427 Parliamentary voters were registered in the town which was always Tory, I cannot help wondering what the size of Haslingden Tory processions must have been. Nearby Blackburn did have at least one Tory meeting attended at that time by over 8,000 people.

In the life of towns like Haslingden public meetings were then a common feature to discuss everything from slavery in America, to the disestablishment of the Church of England and the Roman Catholic confessional. Meetings would run from 6 pm to past midnight with large crowds attending. There were also regular meetings on local matters like town rates, rights of way or street lighting.

The valley of Rossendale, made up of Haslingden and two other small towns, had over 100 friendly societies in the 1870s providing sick and death benefits. Churches also flourished with their choirs, debating and dramatic societies and improvement classes. In Haslingden, where some two-thirds of the population regularly went to church and chapel, attendances of up to 800 were registered at individual church and chapel Mutual Improvement Evenings. The Haslingden Congregational Improvement Society had 200 members paying a penny a week and aimed "at improving composition etc . . . of members by essays, compositions, readings, discussions, etc . . ." Many Sunday schools also had midweek workshops attended by hundreds of people wishing to make all manner of things. There were so many temperance, mutual improvement and political groups arranging public meetings that anyone so inclined could hear a lecture or debate on nearly every weeknight during the winter months. Today, by comparison, such towns are political and cultural deserts.

The cooperative movement made astonishing progress in the 1850s and 1860s. It gave working men independence and encouraged educational and cultural activities through reading rooms, libraries, regular lectures and the payment of children's school fees. Manchester hospitals were supported so that sick members could receive full attention. Haslingden had three cooperative societies in the 1870s and a fourth was added in 1880. During the 1870s the Haslingden Industrial Cooperative Society established a library of 800 volumes and opened five newspaper reading rooms.

Houses were also built by such societies and cooperative mills

flourished. In 1865 there were in the Rossendale valley 18
large cooperative cotton mills with a paid-up share and loan
capital approaching £500,000. In 1882 the Rossendale Cooperative
Mills paid the highest dividend of any Lancashire mills—25 per
cent.

Music was tremendously popular in the late nineteenth century.
Chamber music was played in many homes and there were chamber music recitals in Haslingden several times a year, featuring
players of international distinction. The town also had a choral
society able to muster a hundred singers for its concerts. There
were two small orchestras in the town which in 1885 combined to
form the Haslingden Orchestral Society, which played symphonies
by Beethoven and Haydn. There were in addition in Haslingden
several dance bands as well as numerous private groups of players.
The Messiah was a regular feature of musical life at numerous
churches and chapels at least once in the year.

Outside concerts in Haslingden were frequently arranged by
individuals who backed them with their own money. Sir Charles
Hallé and his band (forerunner of the Hallé Orchestra) made its
first appearance in Rawtenstall, one of the other Rossendale
valley towns, when its local backer lost £40. On later occasions,
however, he recorded a profit. Melba sang at Bacup and there were
regular visits to all Lancashire towns by touring opera companies.

Brass bands were tremendously popular. Every village and large
mill boasted one and there were over 20 in Rossendale in the
1870s. Often the first stirrings of civic pride arose from following
the bands to the Belle Vue, Manchester, and other concerts.
Special trains carried supporters to the concerts and after a victory
the whole town would turn out past midnight to welcome the band
back at the railway station. Thousands would also listen to re-
hearsals when bands were preparing for major concerts. Brass
band music was of a high standard and largely consisted of the
works of the great masters, including in particular Verdi's operas
which were often chosen as test pieces.

Today there is only one brass band in Haslingden, another two
in the rest of Rossendale, only one dance band in the valley and no
orchestras. The population of the valley towns is little different
from what it was in 1868. There are a number of ad hoc pop groups

but the guitar has never approached the popularity of the piano which in the 1870s was admired by all and owned and played in a high proportion of homes.

One illustration of last century's higher cultural standards is that in November 1889, Helmshore Football Club, a village team in Haslingden, gave a "well attended" concert in Musbury National School. W. B. Yates, the village schoolmaster, "opened the proceedings" by playing a piano sonata by Dussek. Dussek (1761–1812) was one of those talented but overlooked composers "discovered" in recent years by Radio 3. Where would you find a football club putting on such a concert today?

There were also far more specialist societies in 1870. Natural history, geology, botany, floral and horticultural societies abounded and Haslingden even had an Agricultural Society formed in 1857. There were also the Mechanics' Institutes in each town with evening classes, sponsored concerts and poetry readings, open to the general public. In 1858 Warrington Mechanics' Institute bought what was probably the first mobile library—a one-horse van, filled with books—which it sent once a week "to every door in Warrington and the vicinity".

Even sport has declined. Only association football now claims as many players in Lancashire. There was certainly more participation in cricket, tennis, rugby, and rambling in any Lancashire town in the 1870s than there is today.

I imagine that the inhabitants of East Lancashire of 1870 would be amazed and shocked if they could see the present low level of culture. They would surely have anticipated that more education would have meant more good music, more theatricals, more political debates, more poetry readings and more cultural activities.

Is it a sign of the failure of education in its present form that so few people are stimulated by it; that they regard it, as do most recruits even to the Open University, as merely a means of obtaining a certificate or degree to further their own careers and earning capacity.

It is no answer to maintain that there are now alternative attractions to education and culture. The distraction of television provides no universal alibi. There were always alternative attractions to whatever people wanted to do. There were long hours of work in the nineteenth century, there was the heavy drinking and a huge number of public houses in industrial districts, there were the dog races, there was the rising interest in town football. Blackburn with a population of 65,000 in 1863 had 54 brothels and places of ill-fame and 115 "known" prostitutes—one for every 220 of the adult male population. The nineteenth century did not lack a variety of distractions.

The difference is probably that in 1870 many people in Britain believed in self-help and participation and felt the release of energy these activities always bring. They would have repudiated Arts Councils providing subsidies. The mid-twentieth century, however, has replaced a "do-it-yourself" community by a spectator society expecting someone else—government, local authority or social service—to solve people's problems and regulate their lives. It is interesting to speculate how far compulsory state education has contributed to the cultural decline.*

*For many of the cultural and social activities of the nineteenth century see, C. Aspin, *Lancashire, The First Industrial Society*, Helmshire, 1869.

PART II

The Reasons for Breakdown

Chapter 7

Retreat from Authority

There would seem to be little use in maintaining schools unless there is a generally accepted view of what their purpose should be. Yet during the last 20 years any such view has become ever more confused in Britain and the Western World. The very form of external and internal school organisation, the subjects taught, the methods employed and the values nurtured imply some view of education's role in society. It is this view which is now in dispute with those whom A. E. Dyson has termed "malcontent idealists" attacking all the traditional concepts.

Underlying the traditionalist approach is the belief that civilisation and learning are fragile plants which need to be carefully protected. The traditionalist believes that our present civilisation and learning is good only because we have winnowed the fruits of 5,000 years of the experience and thought of earlier civilisations. He believes that neither civilisation nor learning, which is part of its flowering, is natural and spontaneous but that both arise from nurture, carefully analysed respect for the past, and controlled discipline. Neither civilisation nor learning is something we can rediscover in each generation. Once destroyed both may never be rebuilt.

The traditionalist also believes that just as no man or men can "discover" learning and civilisation, so no man is perfectible in his lifetime. The Jew and Christian may start from the Garden of Eden and the fall of man, and the humanist may agree that even if man is perfectible it may be millions of years before he approaches this state. They would accept the message of Robert Ardrey's *Territorial Imperative* and Anthony Jay's *Corporation Man* that primitive genes still influence our behaviour. Thus some form of moral law with restraint on personal conduct is as

necessary to protect the individual as formal law is to protect
man in society and as structure and respect for the achievements
of the past are essential to protect learning.

The traditionalist is not a millenarian. Outside ordered society,
he agrees with Thomas Hobbes that life is "solitary, poor, nasty,
brutish and short". He thus has a mission to defend civilisation and
learning while preventing it from becoming static and moribund.
He does believe, however, that man can see further only when he
stands on the shoulders of those who have gone before and that he
is the heir of the past as he is the custodian of the future.

Thus the traditionalist believes that freedom, happiness and
fulfilment can exist only within an institutional framework of law
and structure. Structure is the very essence of reputable and efficient institutions. A school exists to pass on literacy and numeracy,
a body of historical, geographical, literary and historical knowledge,
an appreciation of art and music, disciplined habits of learning
and vocational skills. Only by experiencing such a schooling will
the pupil become free to live his own life more fully. To "free" the
individual from such a schooling could imprison him for life in
his own fanciful ideas far removed from reality. Similarly, a
university exists to uphold and transmit learning, to give the
ability to recognise objective thought, to enlarge the frontiers of
knowledge, and to fulfil potential by bringing individuals into
contact with excellence. A person who does not experience this at
a university may never know the joy of detached thought nor
glimpse the greatness to which he could aspire.

It is important to emphasise that the traditionalist does not accept
a static society or body of knowledge. He believes that there should
be a continuing process of criticism, renewal, organic growth and
development, but that this is only likely to happen within a framework of orderly and rational discourse. No reformer is likely to
suggest valuable improvements until he is aware how and why
present structures have arisen and knows something of what
happened in history when previous reforms were made.

An historian will have to study all the known facts about his
period and speciality before he can take the knowledge and the
analysis of that period further. If he tries to do this without the
knowledge of what other historians have discovered and concluded

then he is likely to be a mere chronicler of events describing sets of apparently conflicting information. He is thus only free as an historian when he has been trained in its discipline and has absorbed its knowledge.

Similarly, a student must master moral law and theology before pronouncing on religion just as he must study the science of politics and much else before he can comment authoritatively on politics. Freedom and purpose to the traditionalist always arise from a mastery of knowledge and its structure. To neglect such essentials is to dash madly backwards and forwards and to risk speaking gibberish—of which there is plenty in evidence these days.

Against this traditionalist view that freedoms only exist within order and structure, there may be contrasted the "naive arrogants" or "malcontents" who proclaim with Jean-Jacques Rousseau that "Man is born free, and is everywhere in chains". They tend towards the belief that the child left free will grow up all-wise, all-knowing, all-selfless, and all-noble and it is only some forms of restriction or oppression by adults, religion, capitalism, communism or state socialism which prevents this blessed state arising spontaneously. Not all millenarians adopt this extreme view but its influence is plainly visible among the pseudo-intellectuals, especially teachers, journalists and broadcasters, whom F. A. Hayek calls "dealers in second-hand ideas".

Some people have always believed that somewhere there is a millennium, a brave new world where there is no pain, no hunger, no sin or evil, and where the lion and the lamb lie down together. Religion has wisely offered this millennium in another world and in another time but the age in which we live, having turned its back on religion, believes that by some release or manipulation of people the promised land can be approached if not reached.

The followers, complete or partial, of this view of the perfectibility of man by environmental means saw in education the grand vehicle for this redemption. Most originally saw it as an escape from structure, but others have built a new orthodoxy of alternative structure, be it open plan, projects, discovery lessons, or reading readiness which can manipulate children to be free. To achieve this release, however, the past is to be set aside, all tried methods destroyed, and the brave new world is to be created as a one-off job in our life-time. Little wonder that Britain and the West have suffered from a youth cult; it is the young who will be saved and the old who are degenerate. It is the almost total rejection of the past which cuts the new millennarians off from the older Marxists.

If J. J. Rousseau's *Emile* was the Bible of this new cult, its spiritual adviser was Sigmund Freud who showed the great influence of repressions on the ordinary person and the need to talk them out. The millenarians interpreted his views as an implicit condemnation and prohibition of all restrictions or compulsions on the freedom of the child either in learning or in behaviour for fear of developing repressions and causing him to be stunted in his mental and even physical development.

These "romantic primitifs" who have part but certainly not the whole of the truth—have been joined over the last few years by the egalitarians, the modern levellers, who, rejecting all heredity as some once rejected the idea that the earth revolved round the sun, see differences of ability or intellect as simply a function of differences in home and social class. They are determined to level them all by taking more and more control over individual men and women—at whatever pain and cost, one dreads to think.

There has been a strange dichotomy in the views of the "malcontent idealists". Beginning with a trumpeting for liberty, freedom and deliverance from restraints, they now demand ever more regulation of man in society so that they condition him in the way they wish. Their aims can only be approached, for they will never be fulfilled, within a totalitarian society of which they are the autocratic rulers. The "deschoolers" will almost certainly move towards opposition to the egalitarians and may well ally themselves with the traditionalists since they too are concerned about freedom, even if they see it differently from the traditionalists. The egalitarians could be the most repressive manipulators of all time.

The improbable alliance of the followers of Rousseau, the psychological non-repressors, with the egalitarians has been almost too much for the defenders of our traditional liberal culture and they have buried their heads. Yet it may be opportune to counter attack, rather than wait until the madness has passed like a fever. The threat of the strange alliance may be defeated by pointing out the sort of schools and society which will be created by the application of their ideas. The precursors of such an education and such a society are already visible in many schools and in many movements. They can hardly please their supporters let alone appeal to others.

The collapse of externally-enforced law in society would mean not the ideal society but the rule of the thug, the thrusting and the brutal, with no security, no rules, and no conventions to protect the weak and the children. The meek would certainly not inherit the earth! It is very likely that it would be the hard-line Marxists who would gain when the system collapsed and it is not without relevance to the threat to our values that Birmingham in 1974 produced a new religious education syllabus where 38 pages were devoted to Christianity and 41 to Communism.

In schools, the collapse of order, structure and external discipline would mean that some never learned even to read or write or develop the talents with which they were born. With no school structure and curriculum, apart from liberation and equality, pupils would be dependent upon the interests and inclinations of their teachers and some would leave school for society doubly deprived. There would be no excellence or élitism in art, music, theology and philosophy. The daubings of a child would claim equal standing with the paintings of Constable, and the graffiti on the wall which did not even rise to the height of a limerick would vie with the writings of Shakespeare.

With no order and no structure there are no values and with no willed continuance there will be no great achievements. Aristotle wrote: "Man without law is the lowest of the animals", and certainly the collapse of authority would put him far lower than the angels. C. S. Lewis summed up this structure when he wrote:

A world in which I was really as good as everyone else, in which I never looked to anyone wiser or cleverer or braver or more learned than I, would be insufferable.

It is in the belief that all who understand the issues will wish to join in preventing the consolidation of such a world that this book is written.

Chapter 8

The Use of the Discovery Method

It is not surprising that an age which has seen the decline in the concept of authority has also thrown doubt upon the function of the teacher and the usefulness of a previously accepted curriculum. An age which stresses youth and liberation sees the child not in relationship to the society in which he must fit and in which alone he can become a full person, but to use Donne's phrase as an island "entire of it self"—surely the ultimate in both deprivation and desolation.

The discovery method is both suspect in philosophy and in practice. It is obvious that a man's freedom and wisdom are dependent upon his being put in touch with the chronicles of previous knowledge and experience. The amount that even the most gifted person can discover in his own lifetime is very small compared with the mass of human knowledge which has been collected over the past 5,000 years. For anyone to grow up believing that he can discover knowledge of great significance in all fields is like the sin of hubris, and nemesis will surely follow such pride.

It is also doubtful in practice how many people are alive today who could discover from scratch the theorems of Euclid, the principles of Michael Faraday's laws of electro-magnetics or even the forms of a language which can only be passed on in nurture. Who can write a Beethoven sonata—and it will take a disproportionate period of time by discovery and archaeological survey or by spiritualist seance to prove that the Battle of Hastings was fought in 1066. It is also a painfully slow method of discovering the law of gravity to take coach loads of children down to Kent at the time of the apple harvest and hope that an apple will drop on the head of each boy and girl!

It is all very well to talk as some educationalists do of the primacy of concepts but it is probable that an understanding of such concepts is more likely to arise from a structured form of learning based upon a series of carefully deduced facts, as in science, than from vague and one-off experiments. The facts covered while one is learning concepts might as well be useful.

It is also highly probable that in practice the traditional methods of teaching are a quicker way of equipping pupils with the body of skills and knowledge they need for a free life than are the pure discovery methods. The tables are a shorthand way of learning numbers and their multiplication and division. Only a very small percentage of our school population will become scholars in any particular subject but all pupils need a body of skills and information for their daily life.

The basic concept of the new mathematics is that all children are going to do "real" (academic) mathematics and understand relationships, but in practice 95 per cent of pupils will do nothing of the sort. This 95 per cent will be concerned with wages, income tax, housekeeping, mortgage repayments, the laying of carpets and the buying of wallpapers, and the relative merits of bank loans and hire-purchase agreements. For most these will be the "real mathematics". A child who knows two times two equals four without having to work it out with coloured sticks and graphs, because he has learnt it by rote until it comes as naturally as breathing, will have much less difficulty with his purchases and other such practical matters than one who can draw complicated graphs of traffic surveys but lacks the rote skills. The fact that he has learnt it by rote makes him freer in his daily life to concentrate on what he is buying or selling.

Nor will mechanisation wipe out the need for our citizens to be able to use with facility elementary mathematical processes like the four rules of addition, subtraction, multiplication and division. To judge by the mistakes made even on bank statements due to the false feeding of computers, it would seem to be a growing necessity for all of us to be able to check carefully our bank, income tax and mortgage accounts.

A letter was sent to the *Daily Telegraph* in 1973 describing how a shop cashier, when given a note for 30 ceiling tiles at five pence each, rang up five pence 30 times. When questioned about her method she said, "This is a stupid machine: it doesn't multiply." It might have been a good thing if she could have multiplied. The ultimate in the discovery method was when one first-year boy at Highbury Grove on being asked in religious education to find the age of a man who was born in 50 B.C. and died in A.D.50 wrote down all the years from 50 B.C. to A.D. 50, added them up in tens and decided the man had been 101 years old!

It is thus little wonder that the "new mathematics" was attacked by Mr. R. C. Lyness, an HMI, in 1969 as lacking the thoroughness, the learning techniques and the firm grasp of systematically developed areas of knowledge. Chemists and physicists have also been critical of the "new mathematics".

There has recently been a growing school of thought which insists that children should understand all processes before they learn them. Applied in practice this would mean that some people will not learn very much and some facts are going to be learnt by very few. Thus few understand electricity, yet this is not necessary to succeed in switching electric lights on or off, or to repair fuses. Similarly one does not need to be able to understand the water circulation system of a house before one baths or even adjusts the ball-cock in a cistern. It might help but it is often unnecessary. Defenders of the "understanding" theory confuse ends with means and for most people education is chiefly a means.

If "understanding" why a process is necessary becomes so confusing that it is accompanied by frequent errors in its use then it might be better to concentrate on the formation of simple habits of calculation unless students decide they wish to probe further. It is likely that many children are less confused by drill than by explanation which is beyond their comprehension. The potential craft apprentice may find it more satisfying to work logs out correctly on base 10 than to build his own confused log tables on other bases.

The child-centred progressive methods were originally adopted as a critique of the old tradition of teaching. As a critique they had considerable validity and were likely to influence for good the older methods. But the generalisation of this critique into a positive ideology and orthodoxy has seriously damaged education and handicapped the child.

The Ministry of Education's Consultative Committee stated in 1931,

> The curriculum is to be thought of in terms of activity and experience rather than of knowledge to be acquired or facts to be stored.

Subsequent to that date inspectors of schools showed more interest in the transient happiness of schoolchildren rather than in their competence in reading, their ability to write grammatically and add accurately. Any facility in retaining information was frankly discouraged.

The Plowden Report was probably the high-tide of the discovery method as it held that the new methods were improving the standards of literacy. The slogan of the discovery method blazoned forth in this Report was that "finding out" had proved to be better for children than "being told".

Professor R. S. Peters, Professor of the Philosophy of Education at the London University Institute of Education, has attacked the derogatory approach to teaching in the Plowden Report with its blunt statement that "The school is not a teaching shop". He has pointed to the wide range of varied approaches which can be used by the good "teacher" including instruction, explanation, the asking of leading questions, demonstration by example, and the correction of pupil attempts. All these approaches can be used with a whole class, with small groups or with individuals.

The approach of the Plowden Report derives from the writings of Rousseau, John Dewey and Jean Piaget, the Swiss psychologist, who claimed that "The child must be the agent of his own learning. These thinkers insist that a pupil gleans most from the experiences around him. Piaget argued that "The teacher must provide the instruments which the children can use to decide for themselves". Rousseau recommended that the child should be surrounded with all his lessons without arousing his suspicions. So classrooms should be arranged with exhibits in haphazard fashion while the teacher stands back like a walk-round store detective.

There is a conflict in this approach between the full freedom for the child where material is laid out in no particular grouping or order so that learning is by incidental and even accidental discovery, and where the child is enticed to learn by the adult laying out material in a specific order. The first method can waste much time. The child would probably much prefer being specifically told the order of the second method instead of being misled by an artful enticement which he could well consider to be dishonest.

Rousseau is wrong to propose that lessons should surround the child without arousing his suspicions. The child is not "suspicious" when he joins school, but Rousseau's methods may make him so. When he gets over his alarm at the separation from his mother, the boy or girl at school for the first time wants to learn and prepare for the real world, where father goes out to work and earns money and mother is a real mother. Never is he so anxious to please and to learn; and to deny him a visible structure at this stage can be very harmful. One of the real pleasures of life is also tackling and overcoming a difficult but graded piece of work which the teacher has prepared.

The ultimate nonsense of the discovery method and its primary responsibility for the decline in standards of literacy is the "reading readiness" approach. The intention is that reading should not be taught until each child discovers a need for it and asks to learn. Some children from literate homes will be able to read and, having seen the advantages of reading before they join school, they will certainly be anxious to extend their skills. Other children, however, from less literate homes, who are not able to recognise letters will not know the joy reading can bring to adults.

Thus if children are left free to choose between a host of activities, the first group from literate homes will extend their reading skills while the second group will turn to waterplay or some game activity and will fall further and further behind the first group. By the time the children from the second group discover a desire to read, much time will have been wasted. They will have become aware of how far they are behind the first group in reading skills. This discovery may deter their endeavours and another group of backward readers is churned out for the secondary schools. Disciplinary problems can also follow, for the non-readers may feel—with justice—that school and society have let them down by not teaching them to read as a matter of course.

Mrs. Betty Root, lecturer and tutor at the Centre for the Teaching of Reading at Reading University, has written:

We are reminded that reading is a product of civilisation, not like physical growth a natural phenomenon. Hence, children generally will neither begin to read nor proceed to acquire the necessary reading skills of life if left to their own devices no matter how rich the reading environment provided by the teachers. They must be given systematic instruction based on an accurate diagnosis of their individual needs throughout their school years.

This reminds one of Dr. Johnson's words, "What is written without effort is in general read without pleasure."

True learning and equality and confidence can best be fostered if children are taught to read immediately they enter the infant school at the age of five.

Jean Piaget argued that a pupil might be 11 years old before formal lessons could be given to him because he may not be capable of grasping factual ideas like number, area and volume before this age. Professor Sir Cyril Burt, however, always held that children could reason by the age of six. The research of Dr. Peter Bryant, in the experimental psychology department at Oxford, satisfied him that small children were capable of logical thought and could cope with more formal teaching methods as early as three years old. He concluded that children should not be allowed to wallow in "meaningless play" but be taught systematically from the start.

Thus "chalk and talk" may return to replace "activity and experience". The teacher may then again come into his proper role. After all young children are not generally assumed to know what will be good for them in the future, and the teacher's job is to teach. Even the National Council for Civil Liberties, which stresses that children should have the right to decide what they want to learn, would presumably draw the line at five-year-old children sitting down and weighing up whether they wanted to read or not!

Practically all research from 1970 onwards has shown the advantages of structured learning. Brian Cane's *The Roots of Learning*, in 1971, showed that children who were *taught* to read immediately they entered infant school at the age of five achieved far better results than those kept waiting for "reading readiness". Firm teacher control and sympathetic teaching of reading brought the best results. The School's Council *Working Party Paper 31* showed conclusively that immigrant pupils learned most quickly in schools with order and structured learning. Most striking was the doctoral thesis at Leicester University in 1972 which concluded that the best creative poetry came from students who were "fed on a rich diet of structured verbal discussion".

The National Children's Bureau's *From Birth to Seven*, published in 1972, showed that Scottish seven-year-olds were 11 months ahead of English seven-year-olds in reading. This probably occurred because Scottish teachers are more likely to put their children on systematic reading instruction immediately they enter infant school. *Educational Research*, however, has published a survey of reading standards in Aberdeen in 1969 and 1972 which showed that while standards had slightly improved at the age of eight they had fallen significantly at the age of 11 During the decade many new primary schools had been built in Aberdeen which had encouraged new activity and individual teaching and the 11-plus selection control mechanism had been withdrawn. It was apparently the working-class children who suffered most by these changes.

Research from 1968 onwards has produced much evidence of the continued success of the traditional phonic reading instruction. The work of Dr. Jeanne Chall in America and of Dr. Joyce Morris and Mrs. Betty Root in Britain have shown that average and below-average children are handicapped by a method of beginning reading which stresses meaning rather than cracking the code by the phonic method. Metford M. Matthews calls the latter "the straight and narrow way". Vera Southgate in 1966 quoted Glenn Doman who worked with a team of specialists on brain-damaged children in the USA, when he said that even such children could be taught to read well by the age of three.

Recent research by Professor A. Jensen in America suggests that learning and thinking are two largely independent cognitive abilities. Many children of low I.Q. who are poor at thinking are quite normal at learning. Jensen has suggested that the discovery method of progressive education makes the acquisition of knowledge and skills increasingly difficult for the child with a low I.Q. because of the demands placed on his intelligence. Many of these children would learn much better where the teaching methods stress rote learning.

It is a pity that in an age of change these novel methods have been called "progressive" since most people like to identify with progress. A better and more accurate title for such methods would be "experimental" which puts them in sharper contrast with traditional or proven methods. A teacher who has a basic philosophy and belief in her function may be called "traditional" while using many adaptations of "progressive" methods without risking the progress of her children by adopting completely untried approaches to learning in the name of novelty. The good traditional teacher is flexible within her approach and syllabus. Her teaching is exciting, her relationship with pupils is reasonably relaxed and close, but she remains in control of the teaching situation. She knows what her purpose is—the teaching of literacy and numeracy in the infant school and a wider body of knowledge and more practiced skills in the primary and lower secondary schools.

Why then has there been an attack on this role of the teacher over the last 10 years with the resulting crisis of confidence?

Chapter 9

The Fashion for Change

In the last 10 years British schools have undergone a type of cultural revolution on the Chinese pattern which has still not come to an end. Revisionism and traditional teaching methods and the role of the school and the teacher have been attacked with serious consequences to our educational and social system.

Mr. Edward Short, a former Labour Minister of Education, said in 1972,

> The teacher has lost his omniscience. He can no longer baffle his pupils with science. No one stands in awe of his superior knowledge any longer . . . The old, externally imposed discipline made children hypocrites and liars because when the disciplinarian was absent, whether he was parent, teacher or policeman, there was no discipline.

Edward Short linked this strange condemnation of external order and discipline with an attack on formal class lessons as inefficient.

In somewhat similar vein Miss Monica Sims, Head of BBC Children's Television Programmes, attacked Sesame Street as "too middle class", "right answers are demanded and praised" and since it accepted the society in which we live it could be called "indoctrination".

It is of possible historical significance that even in 1974 when the tide began to turn against both the large school and many of the new methods that a huge campus school planned to open at Milton Keynes proudly proclaimed, "It is a school with no uniforms, no prefects, no canes; where staff are called by first names . . ."

As in Russia from 1870–1932 we have had all the nonsense methods or non-methods advocated: no examinations, no homework, no marks, pupil councils running schools, democratising of schools, the abolition of subjects, integrated days, family groupings, team teaching, the non-recognition of ability differences between pupils, and the rest. It should be pointed out that in 1932 when Russia realised the educational failure of these continued changes there was a return to a form of schooling rather like that of Victorian England. Russia's economic and scientific progress seems to date from this change of approach.

I am not suggesting that all schools have tried some of these novel methods, or that many schools have tried them all. Nevertheless their influence has been widespread. Educational advisers have taken them up and teachers have been made to feel blackhearted reactionaries and relics of feudalism if they dared resist "progressive methods". There has also been a feeling that promotion of teachers has depended upon the number of courses they have attended and the amount of progressive jargon they trotted out in their answers at interview. Thus the self-confidence and even the honesty of the competent traditional teachers who could achieve best results within a structure have been undermined. They have tended to become either defensive, secret traditionalists or half-hearted converts to progressivism, waiting anxiously for retirement, like soldiers longing for demobilisation. Can this really be good for pupils?

Tyrell Burgess, has written in a publication of the Department of Education and Science:

Generally the rigid divisions of the timetable into "subjects" will loosen; lessons will resemble lectures less and projects more. Formal instruction will look increasingly historic.

He also suggested that the teacher may no longer regard spelling and punctuation as the main subject of English Teaching:

For these purposes spelling and punctuation are aids, not regulations.

This latter comment may hold little hope out for a girl who wants to be a shorthand typist not the rare writer of creative fiction or an education lecturer. But one need not worry since one boy in Birmingham in 1971 achieved a grade 1 General Certificate of Education (GCE) 'O' level pass in General Studies for a 25-minute horror film called *Ashes of Dracula*!

The decline of subject barriers has happened at the very time when the average calibre of teachers entering the profession was noticeably falling. More is being demanded of teachers whose intellectual ability and breadth of knowledge is noticeably less. The demand for renaissance minds discovering their own syllabuses has coincided with a period in which such gifted minds have largely ceased to enter teaching. This decline makes the situation all the more serious.

The phasing out of the 11-plus examination in many local education authorities in Britain has meant the abandonment of a major control mechanism on the primary school. The withdrawal from schools of the general inspections of Her Majesty's Inspectors (HMIs) has meant greater freedom—or license—for each school, thereby enabling teachers to indulge their own interests irrespective of the effects on their pupils. Thus we have moved towards *teacher-centred* not child-centred education with every teacher "doing his own thing".

The Plowden Report included the following amazing admission:

We have considered whether we can lay down standards that should be achieved by the end of the primary school but concluded that it is not possible to describe a standard of achievement that should be reached by all or most children.

We do not need to be told that no one can lay down identical standards for *all* children, but it is surely a sign of dangerous license and not liberty when those in charge abandon the attempt to indicate basic standards in writing ability, spelling, comprehension, numeracy and a simple knowledge of geography, history and perhaps literature which can be aimed at by average ability 11-year-olds.

The methods to be followed by differing teachers or schools could still be left for each to decide, but without target guide-lines available there can be no objective way of comparing the success of the methods used, as judged by pupil competence and knowledge. Under the new system, the literacy, numeracy and knowledge acquired by a pupil can depend upon Lady Luck, and may vary widely according to the aims of his neighbourhood school and the idiosyncrasies of his teachers. This development helps to explain why parents are becoming so concerned about the choice of school for their children. While the majority may wish to exercise some influence, not all can shop around to get the school they want, and it is lower ability pupils from deprived homes who stand to lose out most by meekly accepting placement in the nearest school.

With fewer or no accepted standards applicable to schools, let us consider the differing effect upon children of coming under teachers (and schools) with varying approaches to English writing.

One teacher of English may not believe in (or even know) the formal rules of grammar and punctuation. He may believe in encouraging "creative writing" even if the result is illegible, unintelligible, mis-spelt, with little or no grammatical accuracy, and centred on ideas which themselves are not worth expressing. A second teacher may believe in the cult of the beautiful people, the noble savage, or primitivism, and give no guidance whatsoever in writing or even reading. He may see himself as no more than the observer or citizen's advice bureau of the classroom, simply answering queries when they arise. The third teacher could be zealous in all forms of written instruction, considering himself responsible for preparing his pupils for a real world which will demand standards from his boys and girls if they are to have a choice of employment.

Pupils of the first teacher who do not receive support from a cultured home background could be semi-illiterate; pupils of the second teacher could grow up totally illiterate; while pupils from the third teacher could be fully literate. Teacher and school freedom encourages both inequality and child deprivation, with results that can be seen in the illiteracy figures at the ages of 11 and 15.

This looseness of curriculum control means that each school not only decides how a subject is taught but even whether it is taught at all. Subjects now come and go according to fashion. The introduction of primary school French is a case in point. It was introduced by "with it" head teachers on the advice of "with it" educational advisers. The results as tested by the National Foundation for Educational Research (NFER) in their Reports of 1970 and 1974, have been very disappointing. This is hardly surprising so long as there are barely enough qualified French teachers to staff the secondary schools. The level of ability of some primary school French teachers was having taken (not necessarily passed) an 'O' level French course, supplemented perhaps by a one-day trip to Boulogne. The NFER Reports show that half the children taught primary school French entered the secondary school positively hostile to the subject and that few could read or write the language well.

It is of interest that entries for 'A' level sociology have soared more than 1,000 per cent in the last 10 years. Here is the secondary school equivalent to the introduction of French in the primary school. Both indicate to the educational establishment that a school has the "with it" image.

The breakdown of accepted standards and order in the schools can cause social and psychological, as well as educational, deprivation. The writings of Bernice Martin, sociologist of Bedford College, London, have shown that the non-structured school with no rules, no discipline, no school uniform, no homework, no morning assembly, no rituals, no team games, no Houses, no form classes, no set subjects, no daily programme, no security of personal desks, chairs and coat pegs, can confuse and alarm the working-class child whom the neo-progressives especially pretend to hold most dear.

Most working-class children come from homes with set rules and a set pattern and they find it impossible to identify with a school without either. Rule-less freedom is no freedom at all to such working-class pupils who need the security of known but fair and just rules. Such children usually prefer a school where they are encouraged to identify and gradually develop greater responsibility within the safety and security of the structure. The absence of his own coat-peg or desk can be agony for the sensitive introverted child in the infant school, so that every change of activity becomes a physical battleground with a struggle for primacy in the pecking-order with the weakest and most nervous child going to the wall.

Secondary schools without rules are alien to the working-class, however popular they may be with the middle-class and the school advisers. It is pupils from such schools without identity who are most likely later to identify with thug gangs and football crowds and wear their favours to boast some identification.

The breakdown of subjects has gone to the point where it has been suggested pictures should not be framed in order to make us all the more aware that there are no barriers in life and knowledge.

The development of open-plan schools where there are no divisions into rooms or sections is the school equivalent of the non-framing of a picture. Schools where everything goes on in one huge room were common in the mid-nineteenth century. Indeed, it is said that the noise of the Upper Room at Eton could be heard half a mile away until curtains were used to divide it into four to deaden the sound. As the nineteenth century continued, teachers welcomed the move to separate curtained rooms and to separate classrooms, first round a central hall and then later this century with the hall removed from the vicinity of the classrooms. I still remember how teachers objected to schools built in the late 1950s and early 1960s where access to one room could only be gained through another.

Thus one wonders if the return to favour of the open-plan primary school is simply the restless move of fashion, like the raising and lowering of women's skirt-lengths, or whether it has been cunningly fostered by authority because it is cheaper and thus highly acceptable at a time of lower costs per place.

An open-plan school was built in the early 1970s at Eastergate, Sussex, with just one big room divided by a curtain only for the eating area at lunchtime. The staffroom consisted of four easy chairs in a corner; there was no head-teacher's room, and all telephone calls had to be taken in the entrance lobby. Visitors to the school, including parents, also had to talk to the headmistress in the hall, competing with the background noise of a hundred children.

Primary and middle schools have been erected in Suffolk with no doors between any activities, even physical education and woodwork. One workbench was shared by science, art and domestic science, and fraternisation between all classes and groups was encouraged in the name of social harmony. The doors separating the woodwork from the domestic science area were only fitted at the insistence of a safety officer. The staff finally divided the school up into rooms by a strategic deployment of cupboards (there being of course no stockrooms) so that they could revert to classroom teaching.

The philosophy behind the revived open-plan schools, in contrast to their nineteenth century predecessors, is to encourage continuous, easy, relaxed relationships. The teachers are generally addressed by their Christian names and an attempt is made to develop the idea that teachers and pupils are all equal learners together. This is just not true and the children know it. Most would prefer the honest approach where teachers were teachers and had the dignity of adults. Children prefer respecting and liking teachers to treating them as their chums. A similar philosophy of easy and open approach between staff and students at university level at Essex University was far from successful.

Having taught English in a Victorian school in Lancashire, with the adjacent central hall being used for physical education and choirs, I commiserate with the staff in open-plan schools. In my experience, quiet concentration and uninterrupted study are essential for disciplined learning. I was certainly not surprised at a girl's comment in "Any Answers" in 1973 when, in reply to an observation of Dame Mary Green in favour of team teaching, she stated that with a background of other teaching noise she found it very difficult to work out a problem. Such open-plan schools are a product of Radio One, the pop programmes, and a generation brought up to a background of noise and chaos. They are only equalled by the efforts of one Hounslow Secondary School which, in 1970 for its Prize Day, tried in the words of its headmistress "to create a night-club atmosphere". In city schools—particularly newly-built ones—the distraction from neighbouring roads and factories is already sufficient without further noise. Even to children, silence can be a blessed thing!

As in all forms of large-scale organisation, the individual teacher loses his freedom of action in the commune-type, open-plan school. He cannot decide his programme with his class for the day or week without consulting all the other teachers in the commune.

I certainly know teachers (and have letters from many) who find it difficult to gain a proper relationship with a class when other people are present. There is little security for the teacher or the class in the open-plan school, and the close warmth of intimacy between teacher and class can be lost. I know one capable head of English who could not even teach with another adult in the classroom. Good teaching arises generally from the personal relationship (and shared humour) of a teacher with a class, so that many shy and nervous teachers will be undermined in the open-plan situation.

The idea of the "integrated day" with no stipulated separate subjects is also dangerous. Unless there is strict syllabus control and strict monitoring of progress, there is again a great danger of a lack of balance according to the interests or passing whims of the teacher. If an integrated day still requires all pupils in a class to change the subject at the same time, it is difficult to see the point; and if children change individually, it would seem to put tremendous strain on the teacher. If a teacher had to try to follow the separate progress of every boy and girl in every subject, it must be highly ineffective and uneconomic with 30 children simultaneously on different subjects at different levels. The teachers required to make this work would be twice our present number and even then it is doubtful if the end result would be as good as under the older system.

Fortunately there has recently been a rallying of forces against teacher license and abdication and continued change. Lord James, ex-Head of Manchester Grammar School and ex-Vice-Chancellor of

York University, warned teachers in 1970, against confusing tolerance with indifference and leaving their pupils "in a wasteland of grey neutrality". A teacher, he argued, tended to be "so indoctrinated with the fear of indoctrinating his pupils, that his teaching easily loses all force and conviction". Lord James thought a child needed security, and this included a definite moral code.

Mr. Raymond Maddison, who was special adviser to the Select Committee on Education in the 1966–70 Parliament, concluded in 1971 that there were too many classroom experiments designed by education experts which were of dubious value and that some could positively harm their guinea pig pupils. He continued:

Children suffer by being subjected first to ill-considered experiments and then to ineffectual programmes at the expense of basic instruction. Legitimate advance is prejudiced by association with the less successful projects.

The following year Professor Richard Guyatt, Professor of Graphic Design at the Royal College of Art, said that the concept of "self-expression" or "doing your own thing" had led to some absurd results from art students. Maybe we ought to put the frames and structures back round not only paintings, but also subjects themselves.

Finally in December 1973, Dr. Alfred Yates, director of the NFER, described new ways of teaching as a gamble with children's futures and said that there was no hard evidence that these methods would be any better than the traditional methods.

It is of interest that the great educational pioneer, Sir James Kay Shuttleworth, wrote in 1840:

In some of our English schools a notion is prevalent that a considerable noise is unavoidable, and some teachers are understood to regard the noise as so favourable a sign of the activity of the school so even to assert that the greater the noise, the greater the intellectual progress of the scholars.

I wonder what Sir James would have made of an article in *The Times Educational Supplement* in September 1973, which advocated "twin-focus teaching" (known as TFT) which means "the interaction of pupils with two teachers in one teaching space". It could cause the pupils to squint or roll their eyes while the teachers battled for pecking-order superiority!

In Sweden, which moved over to much more informal teaching methods before Britain, there is considerable disillusionment with the results of the new methods. The government there is under immense pressure to consider a return to more formal methods, discarding new approaches for the old style and even teaching grammar once again.

The fashion for change has been accentuated by a group of teachers who are determined to destroy liberal capitalist society and the so-called class system. In 1973, Mr. P. G. Squibb, senior lecturer at Bingley College of Education, wrote in a publication of the NFER,

Reforms which take place in the context of the traditional hierarchically structured school . . . regulate and support the external social subordination of the lower class child.

A report came to me in 1974 of one London primary school where a left-wing member of staff advocated full freedom for the children to do as they liked, playing tennis, making "water-bombs" and dropping them on to children in the playground. One day he wrote on the blackboard, "Do a drawing to illustrate the slogan 'The Tigers of Destruction are Wiser than the Horses of Destruction' ". Needless to say, one-third of the children in his school were illiterate.

The right of parents to be allowed to choose single-sex schools for their children is under attack from an alliance of progressive teachers and women's liberation enthusiasts. Miss Diana Reader Harris, headmistress of Sherborne School for Girls, made a forceful defence of girls' schools for those who prefer them when she said in November 1974:

There is a constant drive towards early dating, their contemporaries expect it, the commercial world exploits it.

For many girls the single sex school is almost the only place where they can value others and be valued by them wholly as persons with social, intellectual and temperamental qualities to be enjoyed and fulfilled quite apart from the accident of sex.

The right to both privacy and childhood, however, is something that the fashion for change gives little respect.

Chapter 10

The Comprehensive School

Some people have hailed the coming of the comprehensive—the all-ability secondary school—as one of the greatest discoveries and advances of mankind, ignoring the fact that it already existed in the nineteenth century in a school system from which this country slowly moved away. Others, overrating the influence of any school system, have considered that it would not only ruin British education but bring a further economic decline. The truth may lie between these two extremes.

The proponents of the comprehensive school claim that it is efficient, just, inevitable and democratic; just as the Marxist hails the coming of communism as both inevitable and an improvement for which he must strive. While few things are inevitable, we can examine whether comprehensive schooling is more efficient and more just; although it is doubtful if it has anything to do with that overworked word "democracy".

If the comprehensive school is the product of a one-man one-vote democracy, it took some fifty years before it really arrived. But some delay is not unusual in social and political history where one reform leads to a series of others. Thus gentlemen and players at cricket are now treated alike and even come and go by the same pavilion entrance.

Yet it by no means follows that because all men and women have one vote, they must go to the same school any more than they must have the same income, live in the same type of house, or even do the same job. One-man one-vote does not mean that men must be equal in all other respects.

Soviet Russia has experimented with the comprehensive school although one-man one-vote democracy means little in reality there and there are wider differences of earned income than there are in Britain. Since the US has done likewise it appears that the comprehensive school is neither inevitable in a one-man one-vote democracy, nor is it linked with a certain type of economic system. It will thus be best if it is examined purely as a form of school organisation which attempts to maximise the potential of all pupils both for the good of themselves and society. Is it effective as a form of schooling?

From the late nineteenth century until recent years, the bulk of state secondary schools in Britain were divided into two types: grammar and elementary. The grammar (or "secondary") schools enrolled about 20 per cent of pupils on the passing of a "scholarship" examination or the payment of subsidised fees, and they offered an academic education up to university entry. The elementary schools gave basic education, often with a vocational slant, and almost all of their pupils left as soon as they reached the minimum school leaving age. The grammar schools produced the professional, higher clerical and scientific workers, and the elementary schools produced the skilled and unskilled manual employees and the routine office-workers.

The 1944 Education Act ended the fee-paying places in the grammar schools, all places in future being awarded on the "scholarship" examination. This examination was probably the most efficient ever produced. From the research of the National Foundation for Educational Research, it appears that only some 10 per cent of pupils were placed in a school that their future development indicated was unsuitable for them.

After the Second World War teachers and educational opinion became concerned over two issues of the 11-plus selection: they criticised the 10 per cent margin of error in allocation between schools; and they had increasing doubts if a division of 20:80 between academic and general education was correct, either for the pupils or for a Britain which had lost its overseas investments and must now live on its brains.

Arrangements for subsequent transfer between the two types of school were never fully satisfactory. Movement from a grammar to an elementary (now called "secondary modern") school was considered demotion and a family disgrace for the parents of many boys and girls, while the secondary modern school staffs tried to hold on to their bright pupils who should have been in grammar schools. Such pupils were a delight for the secondary modern school teachers to take, and the greater belief in education in the post-war world meant that many such pupils stayed on beyond the age of 15 to sit external examinations with considerable success. The success of such pupils in the GCE 'O' level examination made the misplacement of a small minority of pupils at 11 more obvious to the general public.

The secondary modern school teachers and the parents of their scholars also had a grievance in that until the late 1950s many of the authorities gave more money for books, stationery and games to pupils of the same age attending grammar schools than to those attending secondary modern schools. It appeared that not only were the grammar school pupils more academically gifted but they were more physically active.

Such teachers and educationalists who began to have doubts about the efficiency and justice of the 11-plus selection procedure were soon joined by a body of aggrieved parents. The 1944 Education Act stated that all places in the grammar schools should be free, so that no parents could buy places for their sons and daughters. The same Act had also ended the central school system which had taken pupils just below grammar school entry level. Thus there was a straight pass/fail position at the age of 11.

The middle-class and artisan working-class parents whose sons and daughters had previously taken the fee-paying places in the grammar schools when they failed the 11-plus examination, were aghast on both social and educational grounds at the idea of sending them to secondary modern schools. Some of the richer middle-class parents who could afford independent school fees contracted out of the state system, but the rest joined the teachers and educationalists in campaigning for the end of the selective system now that their own children were at risk.

The educationalists and the disappointed parents were later joined by a third lobby against the 11-plus selective system. These were the left-wing, middle-class intellectuals who were moving towards opposition to all forms of inherited privilege be it hereditary wealth or intellect. This third lobby gave the movement a messianic slant by claiming for the comprehensive school psychological advantages in the promotion of social cohesion, unity and order.

Meanwhile, some of the first comprehensive schools had been operated in rural areas like Anglesey and the Isle of Man where they were a means of building schools of sufficient size to provide varied courses for sparsely populated areas. A number of cities like London and Coventry controlled by the Labour Party then moved towards a form of comprehensive secondary school organisation, to be followed with varying degrees of hesitation and opposition by most Conservative-controlled cities and counties.

Under circular 10/65 the Labour Government of 1964–70 made all new monies for secondary school building conditional on the use of public funds to move towards comprehensive education. Before its fall in 1970 the Labour Government was moving towards the use of greater compulsions to bring in universal comprehensive secondary education.

Soon after the Conservative Parliamentary victory of 1970, Mrs. Margaret Thatcher, as Secretary of the Department of Education and Science, issued another circular, 10/70, which apparently allowed all local education authorities to amend their plans and develop or retain secondary education in whatever way they wished. This was, however, only a partial return to freedom since no plans for new grammar schools were approved under the Conservative government and circular 10/70 did not buttress selective education but simply slowed down the march to comprehensive education.

Mr. Reg Prentice, the Secretary of State for Education and Science in the 1974 Labour Government, soon issued circular 4/74 which again asked all local education authorities to prepare plans for full comprehensive secondary education. It warned that no money would be provided for any other type of secondary school building. Mr. Norman St. John-Stevas, however, the Conservative Shadow Minister of Education, immediately stated that the next Conservative Government would provide money for selective school building and extensions and would also conduct a full investigation into comprehensive school standards. This indicated a much firmer Conservative line but it was a Labour Government which was in office.

There are three tests of the academic success of comprehensive schools as schools: do more pupils come through to 'O' and 'A' levels; do the academically most gifted do as well as under the selective system; and what happens to the children who are least able academically?

By 1973 some 40 per cent of primary school pupils no longer sat the 11-plus examination but went on to comprehensive schools, and this percentage has since steadily, if slowly, risen. Such a percentage, however, provides a sufficient base to examine tentatively the success of the comprehensive school, making due allowances for the form of comprehensive reorganisation and the number of such schools which do not take in a full spread of ability.

It has proved difficult to obtain comparative national figures on 'O' and 'A' level achievements. Professor Robin Pedley, a supporter of comprehensive schools, concluded that in the year 1967–68 in 67 comprehensive schools with fully comprehensive intakes, 20·1 per cent of pupils gained five 'O' level GCE passes and 9·7 per cent gained two 'A' level GCE passes. The national figures for that year for all pupils in secondary schools were 21·3 per cent and 11·8 per cent respectively so the comprehensive figures were unimpressive. Since only one-third of the comprehensive schools replied to Professor Pedley's questionnaire and it is likely that the schools with the lowest pass rates were the ones which kept silent, the comprehensive figures were, on careful examination, even less impressive. Finally, since almost a third of Professor Pedley's 67 schools were in educationally-conscious Wales where only 6 per cent of the nation's children go to school, Pedley's comprehensive results appear seriously over-optimistic. Certainly the inclusion of only one school in Greater London where 14 per cent of the nation's children live, does not indicate a balanced sample.

A number of local education authorities have published figures of their 'O' and 'A' level pass rates, before and after comprehensive reorganisation, which can be compared only after allowing for the steady rise in the numbers passing these examinations nationally. Most such comparisons are inconclusive, sometimes indicating a small relative improvement and sometimes a small relative decline. They certainly give no indication that schooling standards have risen since reorganisation.

The difficulty is to obtain figures of academic results from schools which have a genuine comprehensive intake. In 1974 figures were made available from Manchester and Sheffield. One-third of Manchester schoolchildren go to Roman Catholic voluntary grammar and modern schools and these were still unreorganised into a comprehensive system. The rest went to county schools which were reorganised in 1967 into comprehensive schools.

In 1964 before the reorganisation of the Manchester county schools pupils attending them were much more likely to be sitting 'O' levels than were pupils in the voluntary schools but by 1973 the position was reversed with a higher percentage of pupils sitting GCE 'O' levels in the voluntary schools.

The Sheffield figures of 1965 and 1972, pre-and post-comprehensive reorganisation indicate that while in Sheffield between these years the number of 'O' level passes per pupil increased by 3·6 per cent, the comparative national increase per pupil was 20·6 per cent.

These figures which indicate a decline in academic results after comprehensive reorganisation may account for the fact that from 1965–72 the expected increase of 44 per cent in the number of sixth formers obtaining two 'A' level passes proved to be seriously over-optimistic, the increase was only 28 per cent.

The only serious attempt at a national assessment of comprehensive education (*A Critical Appraisal of Comprehensive Education*, NFER 1972) studied 12 mature comprehensive schools and examined them in detail. The result was that only in five out of 11 schools, for which the question was appropriate, were the proportions of pupils attaining a GCE 'O' level with five or more passes at or above the national average. As regards pupils with two or more 'A' levels, only one of the 11 schools reached the national average.

In the earlier NFER study *Achievement in Mathematics* a direct suitably-weighted comparison is made between the comprehensive school results and the bipartite system for 13-, 14- and 15-year-olds, 'O' and 'A' level candidates. The bipartite schools were superior in all cases and specially so for the 15-year-olds and the 'O' and 'A' level candidates. The 'O' level results for the secondary modern schools were even better than those attained in the comprehensive schools!

It is essential that the comprehensive schools attain as high if not a higher standard with the top 5 per cent of the ability range as did the selective schools since this is the seed corn for the future. There seems little doubt that the standard attained with these high flyers in Britain in the selective schools is the best in the world and that it is this which makes the short British degree course possible. Any lowering of this standard would bring a need for longer university honours courses and could threaten the excellence of our science and scholarship.

Since the Second World War, Britain has won more Nobel prizes for science and literature per head of population than any other major country. In the 1967 Mathematical Schools Olympiad, the British team came fourth out of the twelve participating countries. It is notable that the boys were drawn from Edward VI's School, Stafford, Manchester Grammar School, Winchester and Eton. The first three places in the Olympiad were taken by Russia, East Germany and Hungary, all of which maintain highly selective schools for their more able children.

The more recent *International Study of Achievement in Mathematics* by Professor T. Hüsen of the University of Stockholm listed 12 countries in order of achievement in the standards of those studying mathematics at sixth-form level, and only Israel was superior to Britain. The Swedish mean score was only 80 per cent of the British score and the American only 40 per cent. It would thus appear that whatever criticisms could be made of the secondary selective system, there was no lack of educational opportunity and achievement for the top 5 per cent ability pupils.

Between 1970 and 1972 the number of pupils in comprehensive schools increased by 30 per cent, but their share of Oxbridge scholarships fell from 2·1 per cent to 1·8 per cent.

The 1968 survey of Dr. J. W. B. Douglas, *All our Future*, is alarming in that he found that of the cleverer pupils some 60 per cent in selective schools wished to go on to higher education compared with only 29 per cent in the comprehensive schools. Dr. Douglas considered that this was due to the difference in the atmosphere and aspirations of the two types of school, itself a serious indictment of the academic attitude of, at least some, comprehensive schools.

Dr. F. Rushworth, the headmaster of Holland Park School, London, confessed in 1973 that pupils at his school aged 14 would have been further ahead academically if they had attended a grammar school.

The need for the early recognition and encouragement of the academically bright cannot be overstressed. The idea that they require no teaching is patent nonsense. There has recently been rising concern expressed for very bright pupils who, unrecognised by teachers, pass unnoticed at the back of an ordinary classroom where they buy peace with the teachers and their classmates by contracting out of full involvement and just drift along.

Professor Sir Cyril Burt reminded us that there are as many children with intelligence quotients (I.Q.s) between 150 and 200 as there are children with I.Q.s below 50 and both types of children need special care. He also described how he once discovered in London schools half a dozen children, unrecognised by their teachers, with I.Q.s over 180. He arranged for these children to be transferred to highly-academic education and they later rose to prominence in business, literature and science. Dr. Mia Pringle, in *Able Misfits*, and a 1973 publication of the Schools Council have drawn attention to the neglect of very able children in our schools. One dreads to think what might happen to I.Q. 180 children in non-streamed, non-aspiring comprehensive schools!

The least able also require special treatment from skilled teachers. It is doubtful whether they are as well provided for scholastically in the comprehensive schools as they were in the older secondary modern schools. Their morale may be higher in so far as they are no longer 11-plus rejects, but it may be lower in that they are now the bottom group amongst huge numbers of children. I wonder whether the increased figures for illiteracy at the age of 15 may point to the fact that the least able received better tuition in the 'C' streams of secondary modern schools than they receive in the mixed-ability comprehensive school groups. It would be very interesting to compare the figures of illiteracy at 11 and 15 in areas still selective with areas which have gone comprehensive.

It may not only be the most backward who become the illiterates of the comprehensive schools. The group above them who receive no remedial or "withdrawal" tuition may be lost in large comprehensive schools. It may well be that the higher illiteracy figures arise from this section of our school population who no longer receive in house and year-organised schools the personal security and care of the old form class system.

The teachers and educationalists who supported the comprehensive school shared with the intellectual egalitarians a belief that with improved academic standards more working-class pupils would go on to universities and higher education and educational and social mobility would be encouraged. But it is as well to remember that we had considerable educational and social mobility in Britain under the selective system. Mrs. Shirley Williams, when Labour Minister of State at the Department of Education and Science, told the 1967 Conference of European Ministers of Education that over 26 per cent of the British university population and 35 per cent at all institutions of higher education in Britain were of working-class origin. This was (and is) the highest percentage in the Western World or the Soviet bloc.

The figure of the percentage of university intake drawn from the working-class was 14 per cent in comprehensive Sweden, where 63 per cent were drawn from the upper and upper middle-class, 10 per cent in Denmark, 8·3 per cent in France, 5·3 per cent in West Germany and 4 per cent in Switzerland. In Soviet Russia only 10 per cent of the university intake was drawn from the families of agricultural workers while 82 per cent came from the children of professional families. Most Russian university applicants need private tuition paid for by their parents before they can pass their university entrance examination. When in America genuine universities are separated from other institutions of higher education, their percentage intake from working-class families is lower than for British universities.

It thus appears that whatever could be said against the British selective system, it certainly selected at 11 the highest-ability working-class children from deprived homes (and even deprived schools) and put them in an academic atmosphere in which they blossomed and moved on to higher education. This system, combining the British 11-plus selection, external examinations and generous university grants, seemed to have offered maximum advantage to working-class pupils.

It now appears doubtful whether the comprehensive schools will be as successful in promoting educational and social mobility. Many working-class pupils will only become scholars if placed in an academic atmosphere at an early age, which will not happen in down-town schools which are comprehensive in name only. The reason is that comprehensive schools, more than grammar schools, reflect the intake and mores of their surrounding area. We now know that comprehensive schools are far from equal in their intake and aspirations and most of those with lowest aspirations are in poor working-class areas. We have not got comprehensive schools with equal-ability intakes, but neighbourhood schools reflecting the social class and intellectual level of their areas.

In Inner London the old boroughs of Chelsea, Hampstead and Lewisham had a proportion of non-manual workers to manual workers which was six times as high as in Bermondsey and Bethnal Green. Surveys carried out in these areas showed that the proportion of grammar-school ability children to academically dull or backward children varied in roughly the same proportion.

In Cardiff there is one middle and upper-class comprehensive school, while the others are predominantly working-class. But the most interesting figures come from Newcastle, where the intake of two similar-sized comprehensive schools in September 1969 can be compared. The school in the deprived area had only 28 pupils with an I.Q. of 120 or more, which is good university potential calibre, but 82 with an I.Q. below 89, 'C' stream secondary modern school level. But the comprehensive in the middle-class area, taking in the same number of 240 pupils, had 85 with an I.Q. of 120 or over but only 28 with I.Q.s below 89. These are not, and cannot be, equal schools. One is a secondary modern school with a GCE stream, and the other a grammar school with a CSE stream.

As parents come to realise the differences between schools in the same authority, they act to obtain the best for their children. The middle-class parents buy houses in the catchment area of the better schools, and it is quite possible that articulate working-class parents press for the allocation of council flats and homes in their proximity. Thus the discrepancy between the more-able and least-able intake schools widens until the wheel comes full circle and we could have a system of grammar-type schools and secondary-modern-type schools again. Selection will then, however, be made by the purse and influence, rather than a pupil's intellectual potential. I have no doubt which is the more unfair system for the bright working-class boy from a deprived background. His chance of university entry, if attending a low standard neighbourhood comprehensive school will depend, as in Russia, on his parents' ability to buy private tuition.

Prices of houses rise and fall according to the public assessment of the standards of the local schools. Estate agents and local journalists have provided me with information which shows that, in areas as diverse as Bolton, Bromley, Cheam, Pinner and Wolverhampton, prices of similar houses can differ from £1,500 to £5,000 according to the schools that children from a road attend.

It is doubtful whether, outside a totalitarian or collectivist society, anything can be done to make all comprehensive schools of equal standing. "Bussing" does not promote equality and is politically very unpopular. If pupils spend the first half an hour of a day together and the last half an hour of a day together on a bus, the neighbourhood friendship patterns will be even more firmly established and a school will have little effect upon them. On the way to the school in the morning the pupils will copy homework and plan their day, while on the return journey they will arrange to share their evening activities.

Only a totalitarian or collectivist government would nationalise all homes and allocate one duke, one knight, one reverend, one artist, five farmers, four coal miners, one professional soccer player, 10 labourers, three greengrocers, six clerks, one bank manager . . . to live in the catchment area of each school. It would certainly be a 1984 nightmare. Some authorities have wedge-shaped catchment areas on the pie principle going out from the centre of a city to the suburbs but this involves much travelling. Changed catchment areas every year could help to even up schools but would mean that comprehensive schools could not develop the desired close ties with their primary feeder schools. Even if pupils were taken up in helicopters every day and dropped on different schools by random sample, some pupils would have all the luck!

Patrick Gordon Walker, ex-Labour Secretary of State for Education and Science, wrote in 1971:

I fear that in the long run this socially divisive factor will be strengthened rather than decreased by comprehensive reorganisation. Owing to the parental background, and the attraction of teachers, comprehensive schools in "good" areas will become superior to similar schools in less favoured areas.

Schools have this in common with see-saws: their balance and attitude depend on whether they are weighted to academic work or against academic work, according to the initial interests of the pupils. Christopher Jencks considers that the greatest influence on pupils is the attitude of their peer group. If a school is weighted towards a non-academic attitude, the intellectually-gifted working-class boy will never be given his chance since his whole approach will be slanted against academic work by the atmosphere of the school. Such a boy could well be more deprived in a non-academic comprehensive school than his predecessors have been for 70 years. No longer will he be offered the life-boat of 11-plus selection, instead he will be stranded in a school where his academic interest will founder.

It will now be obvious that the middle-class lobby gains most by the abolition of the 11-plus test. In suburban areas all their children will go to schools which are virtually grammar schools. Their concern for the working-class child in the "Go Comprehensive" and "Stop the 11-plus" campaigns may well have been genuine, but it is their own children's privileges which have been increased and the working-class pupils who will suffer. As with most social reforms the results turn out to be different from what was intended by the original reformers. It is enough to make every man a reactionary. For myself, having lived close to all these post-war changes, my own thinking has certainly been affected.

I would conclude that while in mixed social areas comprehensive schools may not necessarily reduce educational opportunities and social mobility, they will certainly do so in one-class deprived areas. It is also possible that while well-disciplined comprehensive schools in rural areas or small towns may succeed in comparison with selective schools, they are likely to do worse in large towns and cities.

The sharply differing standards of comprehensive schools have not been lost on many of their advocates in education and politics. Around 50 per cent of the 1975 Wilson Cabinet send or sent their children to fee-paying schools. Mr. Callaghan, Lord Elwyn-Jones, Roy Jenkins, Denis Healey, John Morris and Lord Shepherd all come within this category. Mr. Harold Wilson sent his two sons to University College School, an independent day school in Hampstead. Mr. Douglas Jay's two daughters and the late Hugh Gaitskell's daughter went to North London Collegiate, a direct grant school.

The late Richard Crossman may have sent his son to a well-respected comprehensive school outside of London but he confessed "that the London system turns most of the comprehensives into inferior secondary moderns". Thus it is not surprising that Shirley Williams, MP, should send her son to a voluntary-aided London grammar school while another Labour MP, Mr. Bruce Douglas-Mann, who sits for a London constituency, sent one son to an independent fee-paying school and his daughter to the same voluntary-aided grammar school as Shirley Williams. Mr. Edward Short, who was once Labour's Secretary of State for Education, sent his daughter to Newcastle High, a direct grant school.

Likewise, a considerable number of comprehensive school headteachers have sent their children to non-comprehensive schools. Although this can sometimes be explained by the lack of comprehensive schools where they live, the public has a right to suspect social and educational reformers who contract their own families out from the reforms they try to force on others.

Mr. Colin Bayne Jardine, headmaster of Culverhay Comprehensive School, Bath, sent two of his sons to a public school and the other two to a direct grant school. Mr. Peter Bolton, headmaster of Beechen Cliff Comprehensive School, Bath, sent his son to a direct grant school and Mr. T. B. F. Mason, of Ralph Allen Comprehensive, Combedown, sent his son to a grammar school. Reference has also been made to Mr. Raymond Long, head of two comprehensive schools, ex-chairman of the Headmasters' Association and now one of ILEA's Inspectors, who signed the "Go-Comprehensive" letter to *The Times* in 1973 and yet had sent his children to a public school and a direct grant school.

When Mrs. Kathleen Hartley, chairman of the Cambridge branch of the Confederation for the Advancement of State Education and an ex-Labour Councillor, moved to London in 1974 she sent her son to Latymer Upper School, a direct grant school founded in 1624.

The case of Sir Ashley Bramall, who sends his son to the Purcell School, a fee-paying school for highly gifted musicians, does not show much belief by the leader of ILEA in the virtues of non-selection. Mr. Donald Venwell, ILEA's assistant Education Officer in charge of comprehensive schools, sends his son to Haileybury, a public school. Mr. Trevor Jagger, the ILEA's School Inspector for secondary schools, also sends his daughter to North London Collegiate School. These decisions do not go unnoticed by the general public, especially those who would like choice for their children but cannot afford it and find their children directed to the neighbourhood comprehensive school.

Apart from their neighbourhood effect, other practical problems in organising comprehensive schools do not appear to have been realised by their early supporters. Most people now acknowledge that size is a problem and both the Department of Education and Science and the ILEA have moved from support of the 2,000-pupil school to smaller schools catering for 750–1000 pupils. However, such schools by drawing from a more compact homogeneous area could be even more affected by the neighbourhood or ghetto principle. Smaller schools in academically-deprived areas could also put the very bright minority even more at risk since they would have fewer of their peer group in the school so that the top standards could be even lower than they are in the larger comprehensive schools.

It is still not fully realised how much more versatility is demanded of class teachers, as well as of headteachers, in comprehensive schools. To require a teacher to take a fast 'A' level GCE group and then transfer to a remedial group or a class of rebellious fifth years, is to ask a great deal from any teacher. Staff may specialise in one section of the school but they must teach part of their time at all levels of age, ability and interest if there is not to be division of staff on an academic/non-academic or a graduate/non-graduate basis.

Mr. Max Morris, then President of the NUT, in an attack on Mrs. Thatcher as Secretary of State for Education, in June 1973, referred to the growing burden in the comprehensives with the "tremendous but educationally worthwhile strain created by teaching children of a very wide range of abilities." It is this strain on teachers—which may not be all that "educationally worth-while"—that could break the comprehensive school.

There is also growing disillusionment with the comprehensive school in other countries. The Spens Report as long ago as 1938 referred to the Professor of Education at Columbia University who had given evidence that the comprehensive high school in America had done justice to neither the able nor the dull pupil. Over the last few years there has been a move towards highly-selective specialist schools in various areas of the United States.

In Western Germany comprehensive schools are almost non-existent. In France, where comprehensive schools exist, they are on a two-tier system with careful observation, testing, counselling and streaming at each stage.

Eastern Europe, likewise, has moved away from a comprehensive school system. Russia has more than 500 secondary schools specialising in individual science and mathematical subjects and some select for entrance at an age as early as seven. Almost 80 per cent of the leavers from these schools gain entry to universities and other institutions of higher education by competitive examination. The Soviet mathematician Kolmogorov set up a special boarding-school attached to Moscow University for 300–400 pupils and over 90 per cent of those who leave this school take up university places. There are also numerous specialist European and Oriental language schools, even for Hindi, again with early selection for entry.

In Czechoslovakia children are selected at the age of eight for special modern language schools. Comprehensive schools there were abandoned in 1964 and 14-year-olds have to compete for places in four-year grammar schools. In Hungary the top 30 per cent are selected at 14 for the gymnasium or grammar schools where they follow intensive specialist courses leading to university entrance examinations. Hungary also has more than 500 primary schools specialising in such subjects as mathematics, gymnastics, Russian, music and even Esperanto.

The retreat from comprehensive education in Eastern Europe, where it has proved less effective academically than selective specialist education, is matched by growing disillusionment with comprehensive schools in Sweden. A poll in 1971 showed that 78 per cent of Swedish parents were dissatisfied with them. One student in Kalmar said in 1972, "I wish we could go back to selection. There is nothing to strive for here." There was a significant comment in a paper by Professor Hüsen following earlier research on the comparisons between "academic" (grammar) and "undifferentiated" (comprehensive) schools in two districts of Stockholm. He called attention to the tendency of pupils in the lower social classes to benefit more from a transfer to an academic secondary school than did children from the higher social classes. The gifted children from academically-deprived homes were the ones who responded most rapidly to selective academic education.

Yet in Britain the move to give special music teaching at Pimlico Comprehensive School in London and to draw talent for this course from all over Inner London, and the 1972 recommendations by Mr. W. F. Roberts, chairman of the N.W. Sports Council, for special sports schools, are about the only signs of an awareness that we may still be moving towards full comprehensive education while the rest of the world, where comprehensives have been tried, may already be moving away.

It is as well to remind readers of Dr. Walter Hamilton's cryptic remark of 1966, "No power on earth can make all schools equally good but it may be possible to come a good deal nearer to making them equally bad."

Chapter 11

Destreaming—The New Frontier

The failure of many comprehensive schools does not bring their most committed supporters to ask whether their basic concept is suspect. Instead, they look for some further reform inside these schools which, they hope, will bring success within their grasp. They have now found a further reform or frontier in non-streaming—let the all-ability class follow the all-ability school.

Mr. Edward Short has stated that streaming should be "a criminal offence in any civilised society". Mrs. Caroline Benn, the continued mainstay of the Comprehensive Schools Committee, has said that schools "should be encouraged to abolish streaming and similar methods of grouping". The Labour Party's *Labour Programme for Britain*, 1972, declared that it would "reconsider such educationally deleterious practices as streaming by ability". The Trades Union Congress, despite the continued division of unions into skilled and unskilled labour, has also resolved for the ending of streaming.

Some primary schools have always streamed, separated pupils of the same age into different classes according to academic ability. Mr. C. C. D. Kemp, after studying 50 London primary schools in the 1950s, decided that streaming was at least as effective as any other method of teaching. In the mid-1960s Professor S. Wiseman conducted a survey of 44 primary schools in Manchester and tested their pupils at the ages of 7+, 8+, 9+ and 10+ in intelligence tests, English and arithmetic to monitor their progress. These tests definitely showed that children in the streamed schools did better than in the unstreamed schools. This conclusion applied to children of all levels of intelligence including the low intelligence bands where the streamed schools had fewer backward children than unstreamed schools on every test.

The study of Mrs. Joan Barker Lunn in 1967 for the NFER is the most widely-known research on this topic. Forty-two matched pairs of streamed and unstreamed primary schools were compared and their children tested in reading, English comprehension, mechanical and problem arithmetic. On all comparisons, the attainment of the children in the streamed schools was superior and on the average they scored 6 per cent higher marks than the children in unstreamed schools. When she repeated her research with different school matchings, there seemed little difference between the streamed and unstreamed schools. It remains significant, however, that in the first study it was the more able children who clearly did better in the streamed schools.

It has been argued that the streaming of a year group into ability classes depresses the least able and encourages the most able, but the very least this impressive research seems to indicate is the probability of improving the performance of the more able without retarding the performance of the least able.

It is certainly likely that streaming makes the work of most teachers easier and thus more effective. If pupils in a year group are split into a number of classes of approximately equal ability, the teacher can more easily adjust his lessons to the average ability of each class and the work of each class can proceed at a satisfactory speed. Each class can be taught as a unit and each pupil can have 40 minutes instruction and work without being in despair because he is being left behind by far brighter pupils or being bored because he is waiting for the laggards to catch up. This arrangement does seem more satisfactory to both teacher and pupil.

The choice between streaming and non-streaming in the primary school, or even in the secondary school, should depend upon the size of the school, the attitude of the teachers and the type of the intake. In a small school in a homogenous area there is probably little or no requirement to stream, but in a large school with a wide spread of ability there generally comes a point when teachers may find streaming a more effective method of teaching. A four-year-old pupil with an I.Q. of 125 will only be one year ahead in mental (intellectual) age of a four-year-old with an I.Q. of 100 but at the age of eight he will be two years ahead and at the age of 12 he will be three years ahead.

The case for streaming, or some other form of ability grouping like setting, where pupils are divided into different performance groups for each subject, comes out most clearly when it is realised that at the age of 16 the pupil with an I.Q. of 125 could well be four years ahead in mental age of the pupil with an I.Q. of 100. At the age of 14 in any random sample of 100 children it is very likely that at least one will have a mental age as high as 19 years, while at least one will have a mental age of only eight. To try to teach pupils of such mental differences in the same class is surely unfair to both. It was the philosopher Bertrand Russell who once said that to teach very bright and very dull children together was the height of cruelty.

Turning to secondary education, grammar schools and secondary modern schools which took homogeneous intakes had little need to stream, although many did. When the comprehensive school was first established it was often considered by staff as a multilateral school enrolling all abilities but with strict streaming within it. Graham Savage, Education Officer of the London County Council, declared in 1944, "Put them [the children] all together and stream like mad." In the early 1960s, I once visited a 13-form entry comprehensive school in South London which was divided into 13 separate streams according to ability. Over a period of years, however, most such schools moved to broad "banding" whereby pupils were divided into three of four broad ability bands with one, two or three classes within each band.

Most research at secondary school level shows that streaming does raise the level of academic achievement. Svenson's study of secondary school streaming in Stockholm in 1962 showed that the educational achievement levels of the brighter children were raised by streaming without any detrimental effect upon the less able. A similar conclusion was reached in Dahllof's analysis of Carlsson's study of streaming in Vaxjo, in South Sweden.

W. R. Borg conducted research in the mid-1960s into the academic progress of 4,000 children in Utah, USA, half of whom were streamed and half unstreamed. He concluded that the superior-ability children did substantially better in streamed classes, the average-ability children did significantly better in streamed classes while the below-average children scored the same on both types of teaching organisation.

A report of the NFER published in 1972, concluded that while mixed-ability classes "may be preferable for approaching the objectives of social integration, flexibility and the continuance of opportunity . . . the effects of heterogeneous grouping in scholastic achievement are not clear". Presumably this means that while it is hoped that intangibles like sociability may be helped by non-streaming, mixed-ability teaching may not help academic achievement. Certainly J. W. B. Douglas in *All Our Future* noted that streaming encouraged the more academically able children to stay at school and go on to higher education. Presumably if the clever children are mixed up with those less bright, they are depressed by the lack of aspirations of the group and are more likely to be drop-outs. Not much of a recommendation for non-streaming!

The Assistant Masters Association, in May 1974, expressed concern that intelligent pupils were losing out because of the absence of competition in the classroom. It is little wonder that the National Association of Head Teachers in the same month drew attention to the education of the 2 per cent exceptionally-gifted children who needed education according to their gifts and special aptitudes.

Complete non-streaming in comprehensive schools, and there is certainly evidence that Mrs. Caroline Benn and other comprehensive supporters would not even have remedial groups, would have consequences in the subjects taught as well as the levels reached. If all-ability classes were to have anything of a unity and the slower pupils were not to be constantly reminded of their slowness, then difficult subjects like Latin, calculus, physics, Shakespearian plays, and even foreign languages, may have to be dropped on the theory that what one could not master no one should attempt. Harry Ree, former Professor of Education at York University, wrote in December 1974 that language teaching in unstreamed comprehensive schools was a waste of time. "In comprehensive schools, with unstreamed classes, the teacher can hardly fail to fail", he concluded. The dropping of difficult subjects would be the ultimate in non-streamed deprivation for the brighter pupils.

Alternatively, *Contact*, the weekly magazine of the ILEA, in 1973 described the effects of destreaming in one comprehensive school in these words: "Learning involves the restraint of asking each pupil to do their best, and therefore not necessarily to finish every assignment set." I can think of nothing more depressing for any pupil than a succession of uncompleted assignments; and this was in a school which still kept its remedial groups.

If, on the other hand, every boy or girl in a mixed-ability class was taught and set work as an individual any teacher:pupil ratio of less than 1:1 as in Rousseau's *Emile* would be unsatisfactory. A pupil in a class of 30 could only receive an average of one minute's tuition in each lesson of 30 minutes which would add up to six or eight minutes tuition a day. In such cases a pupil might as well stay at home to watch the school programme on television or go out to read in the public library.

Little thought has been given to the strain on a teacher who meets say 300 boys in geography in a week in keeping individual records of each boy's progress where individual work is set. Nor has the increased disciplinary problems arising from non-streaming been faced. How can a teacher make sure that each boy is doing his best in individual work where this is set, or stop the bright resenting the slow speed of lessons where there is class instruction? One London comprehensive school has already reported that the resentment of the duller pupils, who can never excel under mixed ability teaching, has increased disciplinary problems. Dr. D. F. Lowenstein has similarly warned that it was asking for trouble to put slow learning children in the same class as fast learners because of the feeling of hopelessness it gives the former.

Professor Eysenck suggested in *The Inequality of Man*, 1973, that there should be more, not less, selection in teaching groups on personality as well as intellectual grounds. He suggested that introverted children benefited most from teaching machines while the "discovery" method was most successful with extrovert pupils. Possibly, if one divided pupils into broad intellectual bands one could have an introvert class and an extrovert teaching class in each band. Certainly it is little wonder that non-streaming is less effective than streaming if the ordinary classroom teacher is expected to cope with all types of intellect and personality in one class and to treat them as individuals. To ask the impossible is never a good basis for any form of constructive action.

Non-streaming has certainly not been a universally acclaimed success in Sweden. Attempts at all-ability teaching have fallen down when the bright have refused to spend their time helping the dull in a kind of monitorial system. The bright have preferred getting ahead on their own. Parents have also complained of their children being bored at school by being left on their own too much and have asked for more class teaching. Lower standards could be the inevitable result of the move to all-ability teaching: class tuition seems slow and individual assignments boring. Certainly non-streaming seems to have little to commend it, educationally.

In Norway parallel courses of varying difficulty have been used within the same class from grades seven or eight upwards. Norway has, however, recently gone further towards ability teaching and is allowing kinds of differentiation that best suit local schools and conditions. More changes may follow if preliminary claims by a Swedish language project that the "assignment of pupils to instruction groups by skills can lead to greater efficiency and less skilled ones can make better progress if taught in a more homogeneous group" stand up to further tests.

For long the proponents of all-ability teaching made their case on the so-called Pygmalion effect of streaming whereby pupils satisfied the "self-fulfilling prophecies" of their teachers by achieving what was expected of them in the stream in which they were placed. The case that pupils improved or worsened academically according to what was expected of them was based on experiments by Robert Rosenthal and Lenore Jacobson in America. These purported to show that a pupil's I.Q. actually rose if his teachers expected a good performance from him and fell if they expected little. Professor R. E. Snow, however, in 1969 effectively destroyed the Pygmalion argument and the validity of Rosenthal's and Jacobson's experiments.

There is considerable evidence to show that children learn more quickly by the age of six or seven if some form of individual competition is introduced. This was the conclusion of W. Moede and Pearl Greenberg in Germany, J. B. Maller and D. B. Ausubel in America. J. B. Miller showed that individual competitiveness was more effective than group competitiveness.

The determination of the non-streamers to press for academic non-streaming would seem to arise from an intellectual arrogance which has only respect for verbal skills. The non-streamers having themselves displayed verbal skills they are determined that all children should have them whether they are capable of such achievements or not. There is, however, little correlation between mechanical aptitudes and skills and academic abilities yet the non-streamers ignore the former as unimportant. Yet it is likely that both the happiness of individuals and the achievements of society would be advanced if pupils were allowed to channel their energies into the subjects and interests in which they excelled. Then the boy who was good at car mechanics would have as much respect as the boy who was good at Latin, and the girl who was good at needlework would have as much self-respect as the girl who was good at calculus. Such an approach liberates human energies and ambitions while the non-streamer would restrain, disappoint and destroy them.

Chapter 12

The Egalitarian Millenarians

As one of the first teachers to support comprehensive schools, I recall that the early enthusiasts saw such schools as educational and schooling, not egalitarian institutions. We believed that by having all children on one campus site they could be easily moved into their proper ability classes and late developers could be switched without the disturbance that accompanies the shift from secondary modern to grammar schools. We also saw the comprehensive as an academic school where more would reach a higher level of scholastic achievement. We believed that the grammar school, academic-type education could be offered to a wider section of each age-group.

When Mr. Harold Wilson, the then Labour Leader of the Opposition, said in 1963 that grammar schools would be abolished "over my dead body" he presumably meant the same, believing that comprehensive schools would offer a grammar-school type education to more pupils. Indeed, as Prime Minister fighting the 1970 General Election, Mr. Wilson said:

We have now made grammar school education available to all, without this iniquitous 11-plus selection . . . What I was concerned with was the Grammar School education I had and it certainly would have been over my dead body, in any government of mine if that kind of education was to be denied to people.

It is surprising that by 1970 Harold Wilson remained unaware of the powerful pressure group building up in the Labour Party and outside to transform new comprehensives away from academic schools into egalitarian institutions aimed at changing the social structure of the country.

Professor Robin Pedley, in his book *The Comprehensive School*, had already made clear his hope that the new schools would give rise to a new egalitarian society. "They must", he wrote, "be unstreamed; there must be no prizes, prefects' badges, comparative marks or ranking orders; equally there must be no competitions, conduct marks or report cards." Denis Marsden since that date has written, "We must seek positive unstreaming, a common curriculum and teaching methods to promote a new co-operative atmosphere". Joan Lestor, MP, said at the 1973 Labour Party Conference: "The comprehensive system of education to which the Labour Party was wedded was being perverted because it had often taken upon itself the values that it was designed to destroy."

Such zealots would hardly be persuaded by a report of the National Association of Schoolmasters which concluded that a non-competitive atmosphere in schools bored the children and encouraged violence.

Mr. Edward Short, MP, considered in 1970 that the real issue was not merely between the rigorous older discipline and the modern child-centred approach, but it was "elitism against egalitarianism, authoritarianism against democracy". A year earlier he had claimed: "one of the great glories of the modern approach in education is that we can have egalitarianism without sacrificing the gifts of the more able".

But what happens when the interests of the social egalitarians and the "more able" conflict? Frances Stevens warned of the danger in her book, *The New Inheritors:*

It has already been demonstrated that to send children to a common school does not automatically ensure that they have a friendship-orbit noticeably wider than have the children of other schools. Almost certainly such a result can be achieved, but it has to be achieved through deliberate planning and engineering. A point will probably be reached at which it must be decided whether such social engineering is to take precedence of all educational functions . . .

Even the more able at games are at risk:

Those who are good at some things are very likely to excel at many, including physical activity. It is therefore extremely probable that, in a large school of highly varied abilities, such things as games teams will tend to have a rough homogeneity of intelligence. In many clubs, too, like will tend to seek like. Who can doubt that for the chess club a self-selecting principle will operate? It will, then, be necessary to exercise either some subtle restrictions or downright direction in the composition of teams, and to lay particular stress on activities such as drama, painting, and dance, in which intelligence does not seem to operate with such discrimination.

This is a great retreat from the noble aim of developing the talents of all children to their maximum fulfilment. Instead, it would appear that the egalitarians must deliberately hold some children back.

Elliott, a South London comprehensive school, gave out a sheet called *Elliott Evening* in 1973 which included the following sentences:

We intended to bring up our pupils in an egalitarian way . . . The aged lion and the young lamb must sit down together at the feet of future Gamaliel:—the age of triumph of the common man—so long delayed—will be achieved, as it should be through education and not political ideology.

I should imagine that the above would generally be regarded as political ideology, if not a messianic creed, which has little to do with the passing on of basic skills and schooling.

One headmaster of a London comprehensive school said at his Prize Evening in 1969, no doubt with a fine display of emotion and self-satisfaction: "One jot of humanity is worth a hundred 'O' levels." If his audience were aware of the school's modest 'O' levels, they must certainly have hoped that humanity was in more plentiful supply! But why should 'O' levels and humanity be regarded as alternatives? No doubt, when a school is doing badly in all respects that can be quantified, it is tempted to claim non-measurable attributes. If so, it is rather worrying that so many supporters of the comprehensive school now claim non-measurable attributes for it. It is likewise suspicious that most comprehensive proponents of non-streaming also put their case in non-measurable and highly emotional terms that divert attention away from the likely detrimental scholastic effect.

Dr. F. Rushworth, the headmaster of Holland Park School, acknowledged that the progress of his brighter pupils would be slower in their first three years, because of the mixed-ability teaching groups, but claimed they gain in social terms. He said in 1973: "I believe they catch up later. During the first three years here they get great value from meeting people from different backgrounds." I find this an amazing statement. Does Dr. Rushworth think that such able pupils never mix outside the classroom or the school? Are there no bright boys and girls at Holland Park from poor backgrounds? Does he believe that a healthy humility will be developed in academically-gifted pupils by being well ahead in the mixed-ability teaching groups rather than by struggling to keep up with a fast intellectual group? Does familiarity or even irritation with intellectual differences in the classroom make for respect? If non-streaming is so successful in the first three years, why isn't it continued unless these first three years of non-streaming is a sop to politically-motivated governors like Caroline Benn?

I just do not believe that Dr. Rushworth's academically-gifted pupils will ever catch up with equally-gifted pupils well taught in selective ability classes from the time they enter secondary school. Reading-readiness in the infant school is a cause of high illiteracy figures at the age of 11, and non-streaming in the first three years of the comprehensive school could easily be a factor in a lowering of academic standards at GCE 'O' and 'A' level and at university.

True equality means the opportunity to fulfil an individual's abilities, *not* equal treatment of differing abilities, far less equal outcomes. Unlike the "egalitarians", a believer in the genuine equality of men and women will not expect them to be equal in all things, nor will he overstress the intellectual side of life. Instead, he will welcome the diversity of talents rather than wishing to prohibit any talent which all can't or don't have. He will treat all men as equal in the sight of God—and the ballot box—but with differing intellectual, emotional, physical and moral potentialities.

The "egalitarians" who favour comprehensive schools seem determined that all men must be made to appear intellectually able even when it is obvious they are not. Impossible of achievement, the egalitarian in the search for such equality, like the alchemist's stone, could ruin our schools and even make de-schooling a reality since many children will come to find that the egalitarian school has little to offer them. This would be a pity because it would only structure society even more rigidly, and many from poor backgrounds would lose the freedom of educational and social mobility which has been one of the glories of the mixed British system of secondary schooling.

When Roy Hattersley, MP, then Labour Shadow Minister for Education, said at the 1973 Labour Party Conference, "The pursuit of equality of opportunity would be replaced by the pursuit of equality itself", he was moving towards the concept of a totalitarian philosophy which would for its purposes manipulate all its subjects.

The educational egalitarians remind me uncannily of Dostoevsky's Shigalovism in *The Possessed*:

All are slaves and equal in their slavery ... To begin with, the level of education, science and talents is lowered. A high level of education and science is only for great intellects and they are not wanted ... We'll stifle every genius in its infancy. We'll reduce all to a common denominator.

Chapter 13

The Myth of Reverse Discrimination

Writing as Director of the National Foundation for Educational Research, Stephen Wiseman concluded in 1967 that "the argument over nature and nurture as far as general intelligence is concerned is over and settled". He estimated that at the primary school stage 62 per cent of the intellectual ability of a pupil was genetic (inherited), 20 per cent came from the home and only 18 per cent came from the school. Since the home is also hereditary, unless a child is adopted, the proportion between heredity and environment in the making of intelligence is 82:18. Sir Cyril Burt held that 80 per cent of intelligence was hereditary and 20 per cent arose from environment, and Christopher Jencks, Professor of Sociology at Harvard University, and most current writers and researchers would not quarrel with this figure if heredity is taken to include the influence of the home.

Yet we have a minority of influential millenarian educationalists who persist not so much in disputing as in ignoring this hereditary factor. They prefer to disbelieve, with the stubborn certainty of flat-earthers, the findings of objective research and cling to the dogma that the brains of all people are equal or almost equal in intellectual potential and that it is only privilege or social class which makes them unequal. Common sense confirms that such educationalists are plainly products of an age which has retreated from rationalism.

The dominance of the hereditary factor in intelligence does not make schooling unimportant. Schooling is all the more necessary to develop potential. It cannot change children but it can give them the opportunity to be their full selves. In so far as there is generally some recession to the mean in intelligence in each generation, schooling is of still more importance. The children of very bright parents are likely to have children less bright than themselves and the children of very dull parents will, on the average, have children who are less dull than themselves. Thus the highly intelligent are not a fixed hereditary social caste but need the right education to permit them the educational and social mobility which can enable them to develop to their full potential. Social class in an open society is not static but generally follows intelligence.

The privileges of a pupil in such an open society do not come from his parentage except by hereditary intelligence and his early home environment. H. Acland's analysis of the data in the Plowden Report points to the fact that social class as such has no effect on the stream in a school in which a pupil is placed. This confirms the conclusions of J. Floud, A. M. Halsey and F. M. Martin that success and failure in the 11-plus examination can be explained almost entirely in terms of the unequal distribution of measured intelligence among the social classes and that social class membership as such has insignificant effect.

Tables illustrating the recession of intelligence in each generation which were prepared by Sir Cyril Burt indicated that 22 per cent of people needed to move their social class each generation to maintain a stable distribution of I.Q. between the classes. Figures available show 30 per cent of adults in Britain have changed their social class from the one in which they were born, yet critics still assert that the organisation, curriculum and values of British traditional education do not promote social mobility. It seems that no amount of evidence will persuade some educationalists in Britain and America that the intellectual deprivation of children occurs at the moment of conception in the dance of the chromosomes, and not from material, educational or social deprivation.

Max Morris, who as a Communist seems to have learnt surprisingly little from the self-deception of Lysenko in Russia, said in his presidential address to the National Union of Teachers in 1973:

Why did we struggle to win acceptance of the comprehensive

idea? We did so because a divided structure of secondary education, reflecting the social structure of which it is part, is intended to be divisive by denying full educational opportunities to the great mass of children. These are working-class children. That is what we mean when we use the emollient euphemisms "deprived" or "underprivileged".

Professor Maurice Peston in 1971 advocated in the periodical *Comprehensive Education* that university places should be allocated to each type of school on a quota system as if all children were of equal potential intellectual ability and it was only their social class, deprived home or poor school which had hampered their development.

Some politicians seem to believe that somewhere there is a magic formula which will make all men (and women) intellectually equal and it is just the perverse organisation of society—presumably all societies—which holds us back from this promised land. Mr. Edward Short advocated a "vast upheaval" in education with the best teachers assigned to the disadvantaged child. It is doubtful if this would have any effect, even assuming that the heavily-qualified graduate teachers were the best to take remedial education or that the Labour Party would exercise the degree of compulsion necessary to ensure they were sent to the most deprived schools.

Christopher Jencks shows what final nonsense discrimination can lead to when he wrote:

This means trying to allocate the most favourable environments to those individuals who start life with the fewest genetic advantages. By implication, of course, it also means allocating the least favourable environments to those who start life with genetic advantages. If, for example, some students have more trouble than others learning to read, this strangely implies that the teacher should ignore the fast readers and give the slow learners extra help. If this does not work, a remedial teacher should be called in to provide intensive help of a kind not

available in the regular classroom. Taken to its logical conclusion, this strategy would imply that anyone who was reading
above the norm for his age should be sent home, and the entire
resources of the schools devoted to the laggards.

Once academic schooling was a straight race where those who
first crossed the examination tape gained prizes. Later it became
in certain comprehensive schools an Alice in Wonderland "caucus
race" where people ran when they liked and stopped when they
liked but all gained prizes. Now it is apparently to be accounted
"progressive" to convert education into a handicap race where the
ablest are handicapped most to enable everyone to cross the
finishing line at the same time.

Christopher Jencks considers that the type and quality of
education pupils receive have only a marginal effect on their later
success in life and ultimate earning capacity. If all children had
exactly the same quality and quantity of education, he doubts
whether it would remove more than 6 per cent of inequality
between people. Thus to attempt to achieve equality through
forced discrimination in schooling is as likely to be successful as to
cure senility in hospitals. Recent studies like that by Mr. James
Coleman of Johns Hopkins University in 1960, and by Mr. David
Armor of Harvard in 1972, also concluded that better schools will
not eliminate inequality in cognitive skills or economic income.

The research of Dr. Alan Little and Mrs. C. M. Mabey,
described in a paper read to the Sociology Section of the British
Association in 1971, showed that educational improvements for
lower working-class children were only apparent when they went
to schools where more than half the children were middle-class.
This bears out Christopher Jencks's conclusion that the most
influential factor in schooling is the influence of the pupil's peer
group. Thus the eleven-plus selection of very bright working-
class children for grammar school education may be one of the
few successful pieces of reverse discrimination ever practised in
Britain.

There are two reasons why people support equality of opportunity. Some support it to encourage social mobility which edu-

cation has certainly promoted in Britain for many years, although the introduction of comprehensive secondary schools may be causing its decline. Others support equality of opportunity in the hope that it will create a more equal society. This it is very unlikely to do. Equality of opportunity should create a more efficient and a more just society, but a more equal society cannot be created by educational organisation. If people want a more equal society, they will have to look away from the schools to fiscal and industrial measures as Jencks well realises.

Recently the idea of the community school has very much come into vogue in Britain. A neighbourhood school is one which draws all its children from an area but is organised and controlled from a County or Town Hall education office. In contrast, a community school should be not only recruited but also controlled from its catchment area. In theory, it should encourage the co-operation and commitment of an area especially as the parents are a greater influence on children than the schools themselves. Community schools, however, have two disadvantages. First, they can trap boys into an area and, secondly, they appeal to a strange, suffocating nostalgia which lauds and wishes to enforce so-called working-class virtues.

Mr. Brian Jackson, formerly of the Advisory Centre for Education, wants education for children in the industrial North to preserve "traditions of mutuality, qualities of emotional directness, and that intricate kaleidoscope of brass bands, humour, and pigeon fancying". If people in the North wish to continue such pursuits let them by all means do so. But the imposition of a working-class style from outside seems very much like Brian Jackson as the gamekeeper taking charge of a game reserve for a species which either fears the outside world or more likely wants to get out into it and change its skin or feathers from those admired by anthropologists from afar.

The warm-humoured society of the North was an outcome of the hard times and years of industrial depression in the nineteenth and early twentieth centuries, just as the warmth and humour of the cockney in London was accentuated by the blitz in the Second World War. Each were products of circumstances and once their situation changed the people themselves began to want different things—whether Mr. Jackson or the rest of us approve or not.

The preservation of old Lancashire pursuits like bear-baiting, cock-fighting and the Bacup Coco-Nutters (the fore-runners of the Cloggies) would be good for tourism and might rejoice backward-looking "progressives". But probably it would not be so attractive for the inhabitants themselves who want the chance for their children of educational, social and even geographical mobility. The missionaries of the more affluent society have already visited the valley tribes, and the people like their gods. It may be a pity but it is a fact, so that Brian Jackson and his friends will only be able to preserve the old Lancashire in county museums.

It is the rejection by the egalitarians of any belief in a classless "high culture" which is most dangerous. The confusion of their thought is shown in demanding non-streaming and social mixing on one hand and the preservation of specific local working-class cultures as a form of selection on the other.

The rejection of high culture is shown in *Breakthrough to Literacy*, sponsored by the Schools Council, which states that if a child uses expressions like: "I ain't got no milk" and "We wasn't given none", these should be accepted as a natural dialect form and at no time should he be made to feel that these expressions are ugly, unacceptable or bad. This will presumably keep children deprived of proper speech by a false view of equality.

It is of interest that pupils are wiser than their so-called mentors. The research by Dr. Howard Giles of University College, Cardiff, in 1953 showed that teachers who spoke with a standard accent were rated as significantly more intelligent by their pupils than those who spoke with a regional accent.

The best society is perhaps one where people are left free to develop as they wish with access to good schools and full opportunities for mobility. The best help is then self-help. I was confirmed in this view when I read *Born to Fail*, the National Children's Bureau publication of 1973. Here I encountered more gamekeepers in the shape of the psychologists, sociologists and social workers. *Born to Fail* suggests that children are "deprived" if they are born into a family of five or more children, if there is only one parent, if there is bad housing, or if there is a low income. Yet such categories include pretty well all of us born in the 1920s and 1930s in the Industrial North, but thank goodness no one told us we were deprived; and if our teachers had suggested any such things, the self-pride of our parents would have caused them to visit the school and make short shrift of the teachers. We were wanted and we were happy and that is all that counted. It was a warm and caring society. Like Parkinson's Law, the definition of deprivation will expand to include everyone except the social workers and researchers who are naturally not anxious to see their empire diminish.

In Cardiff in 1972 it was reported that three-year-old children from one housing estate were picked up daily in the morning, washed and fed and had their clothes laundered at the local nursery school, all at the expense of the city. This certainly gave no encouragement to self-help, but was more likely to create a continuing state of dependency. Indeed, the whole scheme for increased state nursery provision in Britain, which has been urged as a form of reverse discrimination, needs to be critically examined to see whether it is likely to promote long-run independence.

Amidst the combined pressure of fashionable "progressives", Mrs. Margaret Thatcher in 1973 accepted the recommendations of the Plowden Report that over a 10-year period part-time places should be provided for 90 per cent of four-year-old children and 50 per cent of three-year-olds in nursery schools. This development was assured of a grateful welcome by the teacher unions since it created a demand for a further 15,000 school teachers. Yet all the evidence points to the probability that such expenditure will be largely or totally wasted and could even be harmful.

The United States once pinned its faith on nursery schools to advance general education and as a form of reverse discrimination, but the results were minimal or nil. The children who started nursery school in disadvantaged areas at the age of three or four were ahead of other disadvantaged children from the same area who started infant school at six without this experience; but by the age of seven there was no difference either in attainments or social skills of these two matched groups. Nursery education was a one-stage rocket which went up but fizzled out and came down shortly to the same place.

This result bears out the research done in Britain between 1918 and 1939 and by the American Institute for Research in the Behavioural Sciences in the late 1960s which showed that 99 per cent of the 1,200 types of reverse discrimination investigated produced no beneficial results!

Opinion in America would agree that the support of the mother and the family was the most important influence in childhood. Dr. Mary Robinson, the project director of America's Office of Economic Opportunity, has reported on the success of experiments whereby mothers with young children were paid £2 weekly to attend an afternoon session where they had lectures on child health, vocabulary and development. It was found that mothers became much more responsible after attending these sessions and there was then the critical one-to-one relationship between the mother as teacher and each child which put such children well ahead—not only at the age of five but also at the age of seven—of those attending nursery schools. Mother's care provides more than a one-stage rocket.

How different is this attitude to that of Dr. Mia Pringle, who has suggested a "child-advocate" to keep parents on their toes in bringing up children. The "child-advocate" would be a regular reminder that parents do not have automatic rights to the custody of their children.

It is also interesting that the new American method is probably successful because it strengthens, instead of weakening the family as the major influence on a child's future along with his genetic inheritance. The nineteenth-century pioneers of education never envisaged a situation where the family was weakened. Indeed, when Sir James Kay-Shuttleworth was promoting infant education in the 1860s, he declared the hope that even infant schools would fade away as parents became "more lettered" and less prone to neglect their offspring.

Yet the effect of the British nursery programme could be to kill the 8,000–10,000 playgroups involving some 250,000 young children which have mushroomed spontaneously since 1960, providing at the same time the evidence that the springs of self-help have vigorously survived all discouragements since the Second World War. In London alone in 1973 there were 600 women on courses preparing to become playgroup leaders. As in America these mothers gained in confidence and responsibility while also learning how to encourage children's speech development in an environment of suitable toys, games and other activities.

Constructive relationships between mothers and their children should be strengthened not weakened. Twenty years after John Bowlby taught us what maternal deprivation means, it is no wonder the National Elfrida Rathbone Society opposes the expansion of nursery schools. They are not only expensive, but downgrade the mother for the professional teacher and will be largely if not totally ineffective like most attempts at reverse discrimination.

In 1973 the French put forward a scheme to the Common Market and other European Countries, which proposed that mothers should be paid to stay at home with their children. Such a natural development could certainly be helped by a tax reform that would remove the artificial inducements of the married woman's earned income allowance in Britain which encourages women to leave their young children and go out to work.

Chapter 14

The Attack on Examinations

The attack on examinations comes well down my list of the causes of decline only because it is as yet little more than a threat. Where, however, one important examination—the 11-plus—has been abolished, there is hardly room to doubt that a decline in standards has followed the withdrawal of a control mechanism on the curriculum and standards of schools. I have frequently requested a comparative assessment of the standards in English and mathematics in local education authorities which have retained the 11-plus examination compared with authorities which have abolished it. But so far no such investigation has been made.

Objective examinations fulfil a number of purposes: they stimulate hard work and deep study, they provide an assessment of both the pupil's and the teacher's effectiveness, and they act as an appeals court against the subjective prejudice of teachers or the inefficiency of a school. External examinations were first introduced as a means of opening opportunities to young people irrespective of their background. The oldest known system of examinations was used in China as early as 2000 B.C. for the initial selection of officers for the public service and for their promotion.

In the UK between 1854 and 1870 the substitution of examinations for patronage as a means of entry to the Civil Service transformed standards and made it and the Indian Civil Service admired throughout the world. Nineteenth-century "progressive" opinion, following Jeremy Bentham, advocated examinations as an answer to bribery and favouritism. John Stuart Mill believed that "throwing open the Civil Service to competition was one of the greatest improvements in public affairs ever proposed by government". Benjamin Jowett went further by arguing that examinations had moral value in making success depend on perseverance and self-discipline.

The best basis for the defence of examinations remains that they offer opportunity to all, irrespective of background and school, and by elevating ability and determination as major tests for selection and for promotion they ensure justice is done and national efficiency advanced. Such examinations would be all the more necessary under the neighbourhood comprehensive secondary school system which is likely to become widespread under a Labour government. Without such examinations the well-spoken, well-groomed, middle-class boy wearing a famous school badge would enjoy further advantages over the bright working-class boy in a disastrously-deprived ghetto neighbourhood school. It is the latter's possession of a good General Certificate of Education which proves his intellectual prowess and provides his passport to social and educational mobility.

The withdrawal of the 11-plus examination in Britain—which unlike France lacks an established national curriculum—has indicated the dangers of teacher freedom turned to license. One teacher of junior school English will, as I pointed out in an earlier chapter, consider that grammar, spelling and penmanship still matter, and his pupils will be able to write letters, précis documents and understand both books and the literary requirements of our society. A second teacher may consider that creative essays so long as they are carefully marked are all that are required and his children will be able only to produce carefully-planned essays. The third teacher may carry the bug of creative writing even further, and the children will produce reams of ungrammatical, nonsensical, ill-spelt, uncorrected gibberish. This is what "teacher freedom" with no examinations and no established curriculum really means. Even the monitoring of the primary school mathematics project was abandoned because of the lack of any clear consensus in the teaching world about what constituted the aims of the subject.

We live, however, in an egalitarian age where faith has replaced works and examinations are seen as "divisive", "élitist", "repressive", "authoritarian", even "fascist", an essential part of a "class-stratified, competitive society", a barrier to the emergence of popular culture. The new school of thought is in Lord James's words to be "ungraded, untested and unperturbed".

Mr. Edward Short, whom a Labour Government thought to put in charge of state education, condemned examinations as "a great disincentive to true education, hanging like a millstone around the necks of schools". The Labour Party's Science and Education Committee resolved in 1972 that examinations were "reinforcing social divisions". Meanwhile Mr. Smithies, Chairman of the Education Committee of the National Association of Schoolmasters, declared: "The present 'A' level is socially divisive and very élitist." Anything which grades children academically even for their own good and self-knowledge is apparently at risk.

It is not the inefficiency of examinations which is under attack but the fact that they do grade efficiency. *British Examinations*, published by the NFER, concluded that the standards of examination reliability were "a creditable achievement". A team of dons and students who studied the subject for a number of years at Manchester University concluded that the traditional three-hour examination paper taken under formal conditions was still the best test at university level.

The most appealing criticism of external examinations is that, according to a report of the Association of Assistant Masters, many schools spend more on external examination fees for their fifth and sixth forms than on textbooks for the whole school. This result is, however, a criticism of meagre book allowances rather than of external examinations. Money is well worth spending on effective testing of achievement and potential so that pupils and students are taught at the right level.

There has been much talk of internal assessment in schools and of continuous assessment at universities. The former is difficult to monitor over tens of thousands of centres. An experiment on the internal assessment of English language 'O' level by a group of schools under the Joint Matriculation Board in 1964, recorded average pass rates of over 90 per cent of pupils which was some 35 per cent above the national average.

In Russia where there is internal marking of examinations, the ordinary teacher is under tremendous pressure to pass pupils.

The teacher who awards too many pupils a fail mark may be cajoled or bullied into raising it to a pass, in order that the overall percentage may be high enough to satisfy the headmaster, the district and regional authorities, and the Ministry. Pupils even taunt teachers with their inability to fail them.

Internal marking of scripts, as advocated by the NUT and the Schools Council (where the NUT has a large influence) could also sour the relationship between pupils and teacher. External marking means that the teacher and the pupil are allies, not enemies. Tension can become even more acute at universities under continuous assessment when a student feels he is under a constant three-year examination. Such continuous assessment can lead to plagiarism, favouritism and downright cheating.

University and professional examinations are a necessary defence for the general public. The public want competent doctors and engineers and their university examinations guarantee this. Lord Bowden, Principal of the Manchester University Institute of Science and Technology has written:

As far as we are concerned, the rigour of the scientific disciplines has been unimpaired by "progressive education". If a man wants to learn how to design a suspension bridge or to remove an appendix, he has to accept traditional discipline and submit himself to formal examination before he can be let loose in the world.

In the early and mid-1970s it was the 16-plus 'O' level and 18-plus 'A' level GCE examinations which were under the constant attack of the meddlers. The "progressives" want broad subject examinations over the whole ability range. They are the supporters of integrated curricula and the scratch-the-surface or quiz mentality.

The GCE 'O' level examination aims at the top 25–30 percentile in ability. It can be sat in as many subjects as a pupil and a school decide and it was a single subject pass/fail examination with a number of grades. The Certificate of Secondary Education was introduced as a separate examination, for the next 35–40 per cent ability pupils, but it is now sat (as Miss S. Hale told the Association of Assistant Mistresses Conference in 1972) by some 95 per cent of children who stay on to the age of 16 and do not take the GCE 'O' level. In 1974 with the raising of the school leaving age, large numbers sat the examinations.

The NUT and the Schools Council have been pressing for one examination only at 16-plus covering the whole ability range. That there can be one examination for the 70 I.Q. pupils right through to the 170 I.Q. level is difficult to believe, unless it either bored the bright or brought despair to the academically dull. It would be interesting to know whether Latin and mathematics were to be taught throughout the ability range.

From 1960 onwards there was a rapid increase in the numbers staying on into the sixth forms although this increase began to taper off by 1972. Since only one-third of sixth-formers go on to universities, the qualifying 'A' level examination is now under attack. A further one-third of sixth-formers tackle no 'A' levels, while the remaining third begin at least one. The high drop-out rate of this final third has caused concern to the "progressive" lobby.

It is, however, much kinder to have a high drop-out rate at sixth form level rather than in universities. It is the testing sixth-form 'A' level course which makes the British three-year degree possible. If this course were diluted, it would be necessary to introduce a four-year first degree or an automatic one or two-year higher degree course. The British univeristy drop-out rate is only 16·8 per cent compared with 60 per cent in America and 40 per cent on the Continent.

The Schools Council, possibly in an attempt to justify its existence, has suggested a succession of changes in the sixth form examinations. A Certificate of Extended Education, to be offered after a one-year sixth-form course to pupils who a year previously had gained CSE grades 2–4, is probably sensible if one considers that such pupils should be in school at all. But the attack on the three or four 'A' level courses is much more dangerous. There was first the suggestion of majors and minors, then the electives, then the Qs and Fs (turned down in 1970) and in 1973–4 the suggestion for 5 Ns and Fs.

The current suggestion of the Schools Council is that one or two Fs should be sat, which will be equivalent to 'A' levels, while the Ns will be halfway between 'O' and 'A' level. The aim is to broaden the curriculum, probably to bring us into line with Europe, despite the fact that pupils maturing earlier want more specialisation. The Association of Assistant Masters (AMA) has warned that bright children would be sacrificed to the needs of the not-so-able and the Associated Examining Board has commented that the proposals "run the risk of encouraging mediocrity at the expense of excellence". The proposals would also create a demand for greatly increased sixth-form staffing. I estimate at least 50 per cent more sixth-form teachers would be required, because each sixth-form subject would be taught at two levels.

Mr. Prentice, the Labour Secretary of State for Education, agreed in 1974 with the Schools Council's recommendation to give up the Pass/Fail concept at GCE 'A' level and to have three pass grades on the old standard and two other grades below this, the lowest of which could presumably be attained by all who sat. This could be the beginning of the end of the prized sixth-form standards, in which case universities and professors might have to ignore the Ns and Fs and set their own examinations—unless they were wise and strong enough to demand three Fs and to ignore the Ns.

My favourite quip about the opposition to examinations at university level is that a Society should be formed "For the Abolition of Examinations in Dentistry". An unqualified dentist is not likely to kill anyone, unlike an unqualified doctor or engineer, but he would inflict so much pain that people would quickly be brought to their senses and demand the reintroduction of professional examinations.

Chapter 15

The Fall in the Calibre of Teachers and Teacher Training

Until the 1950s many of the most academically able working-class and middle-class children were delighted to enter teaching as a rewarding, reasonably-paid and secure profession. The great expansion of teacher numbers, however, has meant not only the automatic recruitment of candidates of lower-ability, but the unconscious decision of society to pay the individual teacher less as the total numbers increase and the burden of cost rises even higher. Varied career opportunities and full employment have also enabled many able students to have a much wider choice of career than was offered up to the 1950s.

Thus a profession which could once select has been reduced to taking almost all who wish to join, with the result that its image has been badly tarnished. When Groucho Marx said, "Who wants to join a club that lets in people like me?" he explained why the most selective professions have generally the most applicants. Gone are the days when a candidate, later to become my deputy head at Highbury Grove, would gain his first assistant post from a list of as many as 259 applicants.

In 1970 only 79 per cent of the men and 61 per cent of the women entering Colleges of Education had passed both GCE 'O' level English and mathematics. In 1972 only 40·5 per cent of entrants to Colleges of Education had two or more 'A' levels and only 68·2 per cent had even one 'A' level.

Thus it is not surprising that a NFER Report of 1972, *After 'A' Level*, found that students at Colleges of Education showed the lowest level of academic aptitude of any group in higher education. Mr. F. Willey, MP, Chairman of the Commons Select

Committee on Education and Science up to 1970, and Raymond Maddison, the Committee's special adviser, concluded that one student in every four entering Colleges of Education had no sixth form experience and up to one-fifth were "practically innumerate".

A report of the Rowntree Trust noted that 66 per cent of students entering university had the equivalent of three grade C passes at 'A' level; a standard attained by only 5 per cent of the entrants to Colleges of Education. When I complained some years ago about the quality of students from Colleges of Education, I was told that the colleges were under pressure from the Department of Education and Science to fill all places, irrespective of quality.

Consideration of the subjects studied by graduates who in one recent year took the one-year teachers' course, shows that those with degrees providing easy access to other careers rarely entered teaching. Among arts graduates, some 44 per cent of those with second class honours entered teaching, compared with only 13 per cent of first class honours graduates. Among pure science graduates, 17 per cent of second class graduates became teachers, compared with 4 per cent of those gaining first class honours degrees. Among those who gained degrees in applied sciences, which provided easiest access to industry, only 1 per cent of the second class honours graduates and none of the first class honours graduates trained for teaching.

The shortage of well-qualified teachers is thus most acute in certain subjects, including mathematics in which half of the teachers of the 11–16-year–olds have no mathematical qualifications whatever. Those whose subjects are not a passport to other work, often drift into teaching. Indeed, an AMA Report in 1973 quotes the comment of one graduate: "one gets the impression that teaching attracts the dedicated or the aimless, but never the ambitious". The number of graduate applicants for teacher training courses was still falling in the autumn of 1975 as was the number of 18-year-olds applying for College of Education places.

Morale and self-respect of the profession has fallen so low that a survey made by the NUT in 1969 concluded that half the trainee teachers at Colleges of Education did not want to teach full-time after qualifying. Four out of five students in this survey also considered that their professional training was insufficient. The evidence of the ILEA to the James Committee on Teacher Training in 1971 included an analysis of the views of young teachers serving Inner London which showed that 82 per cent thought that their training had given too little attention to teaching methods.

The present position is, therefore, that a lower calibre of teacher entrant is being even less adequately trained. Colleges of Education in particular seem to have failed in two ways: they have tried to ape universities and to stress sociological subjects with little attention to teaching techniques and they have simply become vehicles for the propaganda of "progressive" educational methods which are ineffective in the schools.

An extreme example of the first failure came to light in 1973 at a London Art Training College which is a branch of the Middlesex Polytechnic. A mature student complained of lectures on drug-taking and witchcraft and of a book list that seemed to consist of all the latest left-wing, if not Marxist, Penguins, *The Teachings of Don Juan* and *The Little Red Schoolbook*. This student described the College as a "training for anarchy" and it was obvious that little or no guidance was given in the techniques of teaching. The failure to concentrate on teaching techniques was also obvious in a survey of the ILEA which showed that less than one in eight junior school teachers recruited had received training in the teaching of reading at a time when at least one in six London junior schoolchildren require such help.

It was alleged by a chairman of a Divisional Education Executive at the 1973 Conference of Divisional Executives that at least one local education authority kept a black list of Colleges of Education which turned out poorly-trained teachers. He named three colleges where teachers were not trained to teach reading.

The evidence suggests that many enter Colleges of Education only because their qualifications are too low to gain a university place. These students attempt to obtain a degree at their college and then end any pretence to become teachers. A London University 1969 report covering its B.Ed degree for Colleges of

Education noted that half the recipients of this degree wanted to do research, not teaching.

A further source of declining standards has been the increased turnover of teachers due to poor salaries, increased disciplinary problems in schools and general discontent. Between 1938–1968 the purchasing power of the salaries of teachers, dons and general practitioners fell by 10 per cent, while the purchasing power of miners, porters and agricultural labourers' wages rose by 25 per cent. The relative purchasing power of teachers' salaries fell further after 1968. In 1965 it took a non-graduate teacher four years to reach the average manual worker's wage, while in 1971 it took eight years and in 1973, ten years. Even for a graduate, it took four years in 1973 to reach the average manual worker's wage. The Houghton Committee recommendations of December, 1974 for increases of between 16 and 32 per cent in teachers' salaries will at least do something temporarily to raise the financial position of teachers.

In Italy a non-graduate teacher starts teaching at a salary 10 per cent ahead of the average manual worker's wage. The take-home pay of a newly-trained Russian teacher, however, is under 80 roubles a month and it is many years before he approaches the average wage of 130 roubles. The respect with which teachers are held in Russia may be some compensation for their poor pay, but there is no such consolation for teachers in Britain where it is money that therefore matters most. The Economic Research Unit in 1970 found that four out of ten sixth-formers who wished to teach decided against it because of the low pay.

The average annual wage of a teacher in Britain in mid-1974 was some £2,400, £7 a week above the average manual wage. This average embraces the teachers earning more than the basic scale, including heads, deputies and all the five scales of special responsibility holders. To obtain these higher scales, teachers have generally to move and 21 per cent do move schools every year, a figure which rises to 30 per cent in London. This clearly does not improve the quality of settled schooling.

The economics of teacher training in Britain are the economics of Passchendaele. After a three-year course costing some £3,000, 80 per cent of the trained women teachers and one-third of the trained male teachers leave within the first six years. Only 20 per cent of the women leavers resign for "involuntary reasons", like childbirth. The majority leave because they do not like teaching or because they have found something more financially rewarding or more interesting to occupy their time. Teaching must be one of the few professions where the majority of the trained personnel are not practising at any time.

The reduction of the pupil-teacher ratio, irrespective of teacher quality, has done untold harm to the teaching profession in Britain. There is, in any case, no evidence for the effectiveness of smaller classes but, since teachers are paid the same irrespective of the number in a class, it is little wonder that they prefer smaller classes. The research of the National Children's Bureau into the 11,000 children born in the same week in 1958, showed that children in classes over 40 did consistently better at reading and arithmetic than children in classes of below 30. Successive researches—by the European Organisation for Economic Cooperation and Development, by Dr. Alan Little in his British Association Paper 1971, by Joyce Morris in her *Standards and Progress in Reading*, and dozens of others—have reinforced this conclusion. Larger classes probably bring children to stimulate each other by questions and by competition, while teachers are forced to use the more effective traditional teaching methods instead of the ineffective "progressive" methods.

Between 1900 and 1971, the number of teachers more than trebled to 428,000, 20 per cent of whom were graduates. Even between 1966–74 the pupil:teacher ratio fell from 28·0 to 25·5 in primary schools and from 18·4 to 17·2 in secondary schools. In addition to encouraging smaller, less effective classes, the additional teachers are increasingly used on administrative and pastoral duties rather than in effective teaching.

The declining purchasing power of teachers' salaries and the fall in the respect in which they are generally held has increased the unionisation of teachers. Both the National Union of Teachers and the National Association of Schoolmasters have become more militant. While the NAS has adopted certain aspects of a militant but respectable trade union, the NUT has tended to become militant for causes not directly educational. There has been a battle for political control of the NUT between an old guard and the left-wingers. Many of the NUT members resigned because of its slant, which coincided with a higher subscription. The Professional Association of Teachers was formed with 8,000 members as a non-striking professional defence body. The NUT attempted to improve its image by ending its Young Teachers Conference which was coming under the control of the New Left. The militancy of the NUT has also strengthened the Joint Four Professional Associations which have some 50,000 members and largely represent the more highly-qualified teachers.

While half the membership of the NUT is below the age of 35, two-thirds of the teachers in London are below 35 and one-third are below 25. This has both increased the teacher militancy and the Rank and File movement and the disciplinary problems of the schools. Many such teachers, while pretending to protect the child, have taken every opportunity to strike and attack "the system". This is why so many London schools were on part-time schooling in 1973 and 1974. Schools have been disrupted and children have even been sent home regularly to allow for a percentage of the staff to be away ill, whether they were ill or not. This has brought a once great teaching profession to its nadir.

The Labour controlled ILEA has tried to play along with the militant teachers. In April 1974 it suggested that schools should work shorter hours and close by 2 pm so that teachers would be paid while they were on strike demonstrations. The ILEA Chairman has been seen to march with demonstrating teachers. No wonder that with internal disciplinary problems and such an attitude by the employers, at least 25 ILEA headteachers resigned in 1974. Mr. Colin Wilcocks retired as head of Clissold Park Comprehensive at the age of 58, declaring that being a London head was "simply not worth the candle".

ILEA, even with its teacher vacancies and absentees, has proportionately more staff than the rest of the country so that there would have been no need to send one pupil home if the teachers had been allocated where they were needed. In 1974 there was one ILEA primary school teacher for every 21·8 pupils compared with an average of one to 25·5 for the whole country. In secondary schools there was one ILEA teacher to 14·6 pupils compared with one to 17·2 nationally. If the secondary school ratio between pupils and teachers in ILEA was increased to the national average, they would need 1,259 fewer teachers; and yet the largest ILEA vacancy shortage of teachers in primary and secondary schools never topped 700! The shortage was thus artificial.

It would appear that the ILEA has failed to fulfil its statutory duty. When the 1944 Education Act clearly laid down "the duty of every local authority to secure that there shall be available for every area sufficient schools ... for providing secondary education", the reference is plainly to full-time education. This duty the ILEA and certain other London boroughs have not fulfilled.

With strikes and walk-outs by teachers in London, it is no wonder that children play truant and the standards of our society fall further. It is symptomatic that the NUT demonstration of July 1974 was joined by 200 National Union of School Student members. The crisis in London is a crisis of standards and the way schools should be run and administered, not the number of teachers. With the decline of teacher standards it is thus little wonder that according to Urie Bronfenbrenner in his *Two Worlds of Children*, British children are the most ill-mannered, undisciplined and selfish in the world.

Chapter 16

The Over-expansion of Universities

The rapid post-Second World War expansion of universities and higher education, which has multiplied the university undergraduate population five-fold since 1945, was a product of a number of factors. There was the generally accepted idea that education was in itself such a good thing that a country could not have too much of it. There was the economic "investment" view that, to compete with other nations, Britain would need a more educated populace or risk being left behind in the race for growth. There was, finally, the strange political idea that, just as comprehensive schools would further the move to a more equal society, an increase in the percentage of students going on to higher education would prove the democratic temper of the country.

The Robbins Report of 1963 encouraged further university expansion by recommending that university places should be provided for 53 per cent of the pupils gaining two 'A' levels. It was based on a simple statistical projection which ignored student motivation. Nor did it assess whether the increasing number of pupils sitting 'A' levels might have lowered this standard so long as the same percentage were being passed by the examining boards. Finally, too little thought was given to the danger that rapid university expansion could mean the recruitment of university lecturers whose qualifications and perhaps attitudes would not have gained them interviews for university appointments in the 1930s and 1940s.

It is also remarkable that no attention was paid to the obvious likelihood that, as with schools, doubling and trebling in size would transform the nature and quality of what we had known as "universities". For instance, while it could be presumed that the small numbers of outstanding dons should spend half their time in research, such an activity would be diluted out of all recognition if the numbers of university teachers were rapidly increased. Topics of research would become trivialised to a point that research itself became suspect.

By the early 1970s there were already signs that university expansion in Britain had happened too quickly or gone too far. In 1972 there were 3,033 and in 1973 2,700 empty places in universities including almost every subject except medicine and dentistry. Demand for university places had fallen relatively so that it was estimated that, of applicants gaining minimum qualifications for university entry and prepared to go to clearing house, 93 per cent in science, 88 per cent in arts, and 92 per cent in engineering gained university places.

It therefore appears that university numbers have already been over-expanded and the quality of entrants diluted. Indeed Mr. L. R. Fletcher, secretary of the University Grants Committee, warned that there could be 7,000 vacant science places by 1977 if there was no cutback in the projected expansion. Further evidence is provided by the fact that, in 1971, the polytechnics spent £10,000 in two weeks advertising their student vacancies in *The Observer* and that one polytechnic spent £8,000 in advertising its image on television and in newspapers. In September 1974 the universities had even to advertise collectively vacancies in 15 subjects which were undersubscribed. Dr. George Tolley, Principal of Sheffield Polytechnic said in 1974 that there were more places in higher education than were needed.

In Britain sixth form expansion has fallen below the numbers which had been expected. Between 1962 and 1970 the number sitting 'A' levels rose by 8·4 per cent a year but then the increase fell off. In 1971 there was a shortfall of 11 per cent in the number sitting 'A' levels, compared with the number estimated in the Department of Education and Science Planning Paper No. 2 of 1970. The science figures in particular were still falling, despite the inclusion of subjects like metalwork which had previously been listed as technical.

These developments reflected a growing public awareness that expansion had gone too far. Probably the first sign of the turn of

the tide was a leader in *The Times* (4th December 1969), entitled
"More Means Worse". Lord Todd, in his presidential address
to the British Association in 1970 said, "I do not believe that this
type of university education is appropriate for such a large
proportion of each age group; it was designed to deal with a small
minority of our young people which were believed to be creative
and to have powers of leadership." So much for the simple-
minded statistics of the Robbins Report. In the same year an
Oxford Joint Committee expressed doubts on future expansion
and held that many of those applying for honours courses would
be better in other forms of higher education.

Lord Annan, Provost of University College, London, warned in
March 1973 that the expansion of student numbers over the next
10 years would mean lower standards. He added that the new
undergraduates:

will largely consist of boys and girls who will probably have
some difficulty in getting a lower second or a third in the
courses which we now offer.

The old sixth former, understood what coming to a
university meant and was prepared to follow a scholarly
discipline.

but the new and expanded intake of the seventies are going to
ask for something different—that something which they call
"relevant".

The new intake would in other words not really understand what
a university was about or was for and looked for instant slogans,
instant hedonism and instant solutions, not scholarship and objective detachment. Not for them the pursuit of intellectual excellence and the inculcation of respect for learning itself.

Dr. Frank Thistlethwaite, Vice-Chancellor of East Anglia

University, said in May 1974 that he did not think that the university had "a firm enough academic base from which to launch further rapid expansion". Sir Geronwy Daniel, Principal of University College, Aberystwyth, also said in the same year that he did not want to meet the University Grants Committee target for his college as it was "neither desirable nor necessary".

There was also a growing view that more students should take courses that were more vocationally-orientated towards an end product. This was why emphasis began to switch from the universities to the polytechnics with their more practical training for employment. Dr. Henry Miller, Vice-Chancellor of Newcastle University, said in January 1974:

I think some of these courses, especially at the newer universities, are out of touch with social needs. Universities must serve a social function, otherwise the issue becomes just self-indulgence . . . I think all courses should train for something. Universities need a strong basis of courses leading to professional skills.

He believed that students were happier reading for one of the professions than taking on "arts for arts' sake" courses.

The same month saw Sir William Alexander, secretary of the Association of Education Committees, arguing that "many university students would be better off on sandwich courses related to their future careers than at a university". In other words, if students did not find a traditional university course relevant, they should not try to overturn it but seek relevance elsewhere in job training.

The fall in demand for university places applied not only to the United Kingdom, but to a number of other "Western" countries. Even in New Zealand there were 900 fewer university students in 1973 than in 1972.

Sweden had decided in 1972 that university departments should be expanded not according to the whims and fashions of students but according to the future demand for subject specialists in the labour market. This would mean that courses would be more vocationally-orientated and there would be less danger of unemployed graduates with a grievance against society because their enjoyable university course had no "relevance" to the outside world. Sweden also became more realistic in its attitude to universities by giving preference in entry to students living at home and to those who had spent at least one year in employment after they left school.

The idea that universities promoted economic growth or that graduates were of direct service to a country's prosperity did considerable harm. It made many undergraduates feel part of an industrial machine, against which they rebelled. It was also wrong. Ernest Rudd had written in *Minerva* in 1968 that an absolute cut in the numbers engaged in postgraduate research on pure science would be an advantage to an individual country. Most such studies, argued Rudd, had no direct application and it was economically more useful just to train technologists, applied scientists and skilled librarians, who could assemble for the applied scientists the findings of pure science research from all over the world.

The suppressed UNESCO Huberman Report pointed out that there was no link between the expenditure on education and economic growth. Indeed, if there were such a link, Germany would have been less economically successful than very many European countries who spent a larger share of their gross national product on education. The United Arab Republic should also have overtaken the United Kingdom, since it had more graduates per head of population.

Unemployed graduates could also be a threat to the social peace of the system which overproduced them. The bloodshed in Sri Lanka (Ceylon) in 1971 largely arose from thousands of disenchanted Guevarist arts graduates. The first graduate shop-stewards linked with industrial unrest also appeared on the British scene in 1973. An indication of the likely degree of graduate unemployment or underemployment can be seen from the 100,000 graduates who applied in 1973 for the 17 vacancies for social education officers advertised by the West Bengal Government.

Because the rapid university expansion was also highly expensive, quality was further sacrificed by enforced economies. One by-product was that the living standards of students fell, which gave them a genuine grievance.

Public Expenditure on Higher Education 1938-1981/2 (*£ million*)

	Universities	Training colleges/ Colleges of Education	Advanced further education	Total
1938	3.6			
1961/62	112			
1967	249	83	71	403
1971/72	300	98	107	505
1981/82 (projected)	573	97	186	856

In 1937–38 the public expenditure on universities was only £3,600,000 but by 1961 it had risen to £112 million. Public expenditure had not only greatly increased, but had come to account for 90 per cent or more of total university finance. In 1937–38 half of the universities' total current and capital expenditure was met from non-government sources. In 1967 only 6 per cent of university expenditure came from such sources. The proportion of expenditure covered by student "fees" (mostly paid by local authorities) had fallen from 25–30 per cent in 1937–38 to only 4 per cent in 1967.

Such dependence on state subventions must have a number of results. Governments would be increasingly bound to judge universities by their economic usefulness and pressure for central coordination, uniformity and accountability was bound to intensify. The public as rate and taxpayers would also come to be more critical of universities and readier to resent lax or deviant behaviour by lecturers or students.

It would probably be best if universities were financed by a more equal mixture of public and private money. Adam Smith criticised endowments as leading to idleness and irrelevant teaching but would *The Wealth of Nations* have been written if he had not enjoyed some endowment backing?

The pressure on the public purse of university expansion in an age of inflation has meant that the purchasing power of student grants has been reduced and fewer students have the benefit of university accommodation. In the decade to 1970 the value of student grants fell by 11–16 per cent against the retail price index or by 20–25 per cent measured against what students are presumed to spend their money on. Part of the grants no longer cover the costs assigned to them, as for example the allowance for halls of residence which is often £60–80 below their cost. According to a survey made by the NUS in 1972, 78 per cent of students living in halls of residence had to pay more than the £240 which the grant apportions to cover this part of their outlay. It is little wonder that there are student discontent and sit-ins.

A survey of Scottish students at Edinburgh University in 1974 showed that students do best either living at home or in halls of residence and not in lodgings. Yet it has become fashionable not to live at home and to complain about the restrictions imposed by halls of residence. Up to the 1960s, the British government accepted the argument that residential universities like Oxford and Cambridge had distinct advantages and financed the building elsewhere of university halls of residence. With increasing financial stringency, this aid was cut back to 25 per cent of costs. Meanwhile, the upgrading of the Colleges of Advanced Technology into universities and the creation of the polytechnics as national institutions reduced the proportion of all students living in residences. Some two in five university students were in residence in 1973, compared with one in 13 of polytechnic students.

The British public and government have also become concerned about the number of state-financed graduates who emigrate after graduating. Some 50 per cent of the 1967 crop of graduate engineers emigrated and one-fifth of the number of medical graduates regularly emigrate. The proportion of graduates emigrating is now four times higher than the proportion for the population as a whole.

There has also been increasing concern about public money backing research which seemed particularly pointless. In 1973

Essex received £16,000 from a Social Science Research Council for a study of what sways a publisher to publish a book!

Yet in the face of increasing problems and frustration, a section of the Labour Party, like believers in some Messianic religion, goes on supporting expansion and open entry to universities which must make them even more overcrowded and purposeless.

Mr. Edward Short said in August 1971, "Can the ivory towers [universities] continue to refuse access to all who wish to enter their walls much longer."? Two years previously he had said, "I myself share the view ... that, eventually, we will have comprehensive universities as well."

Christopher Price, MP, ex-junior minister at the Department of Education and Science, told the 1970 Labour Party conference:

> If the eleven-plus examination was wrong so was the fourteen-plus, the sixteen-plus, the eighteen-plus and the filtering and selection mechanism for university and higher level education ... Miss Jennie Lee had produced the right answer by starting the Open University with no entry qualifications. The principle of the Open University should be applied to the whole of the higher education system and the Labour Party should adopt the slogan of higher education for all.

Dick Scorer, ex-Labour Party Parliamentary Candidate and a Professor of Mathematics at London University, told the same Labour Party conference: "The eighteen-plus examinations were just as bad as the eleven-plus and so were the degree examinations."

The practical consequences of open entry are illustrated by the City University of New York which by 1973 had 260,000 students. Because thousands of students cannot read or write properly, the university had to spend £12 million on preliminary instruction in reading, writing and arithmetic for its new students. New subjects had also to be introduced to enable the less able to cope.

It is probable, however, that a combination of economic stringency and falling applications may enforce a return to reality in the university and higher educational scene. In 1972 there had been talk of a million students in higher education by 1981. The Conservative Government's White Paper of December 1972 cut this figure to 750,000. In January 1974 financial stringency caused the Conservative Government to cut the target further to 700,000 and this was steadily reduced to 640,000 by the Labour Government, in November 1974, taking advantage of a steep fall in the birthrate. It is an ill wind that blows no one any good and economic stringency could cause Britain to reassess the role of higher education and both its damaging dependence on governmental finance and its belief in continued expansion.

Chapter 17

The Revolution That Never Was: The Visual and Electronic Cult

I remember as a schoolboy the novelty, if not the effectiveness, of the rare school sound broadcast, generally on nature, and about birds that did not even exist on our bleak Lancashire hills.

In the middle 1960s there was a belief that we were on the threshold of an electronic revolution in schools and that radio, television, film, language laboratories, computer terminals and teaching machines would turn the teacher into a mechanic-cum-counsellor. The University of Utah was even to develop its continuous progress plan with the counsellor-teachers being advised by computers when students fell below their targets.

After 10 years little of real purpose seems to have happened. Mr. J. H. Munday, a senior inspector of the Department of Education and Science, said in September 1973:

There is no firm evidence to show any massive advance in the effectiveness of teaching by the use of technological methods. Nor is there any evidence that the use of technical devices has produced a major saving in either money or manpower.

Sir Alec Clegg, then Chief Education Officer for the West Riding of Yorkshire, said with his usual shrewd humanity in July 1972 that mechanical teaching aids to learning were an American "contagion" since they could not provide the concern, the praise and the recognition given by a teacher. A pupil certainly cannot proudly bring an apple or some flowers for a machine, but he can seriously lower its efficiency by the clever or even ham-fisted use of a paper clip and a piece of chewing-gum.

It was part of the romantic idea which saw all children as naturally good and eager to learn, which held that children would sit peacefully in front of television sets absorbing knowledge with no one to keep them in order. The machine whch disciplines a boy when he pushes his neighbour off his seat has not yet been invented.

In the United States the average child spends 5,000 hours watching TV at home before he spends an hour at school and while he is at school he will watch for at least a further 10,000 hours in the evenings and weekends, which is almost twice as long a time as he will attend school activities. He watches for entertainment more than instruction and will not necessarily welcome more of it at school in the daytime. He is unlikely to pay the close attention to it that he is expected to pay to school lessons.

New York has spent a huge sum of money on mechanical aids since the war, while its schools have rapidly spiralled downwards. Children there from deprived homes will certainly not be impressed by mechanical aids in school when outside they are surrounded by electronic games parlours, the ubiquitous TV, cars and electric trains. Only dedicated human teachers can do something for them.

In 1968 the ILEA established a closed-circuit television service in London covering 1,370 colleges and schools with a potential audience of 880,000. Sets were put in all schools at considerable expense and the authority produced its own programmes. It is doubtful, however, if the expenditure was as fruitful as the same amount spent on additional books and writing material.

Some of the teacher-producers employed by the ILEA TV service see their aims as destroying schools and teaching, not helping schools. One said in 1972 (*The Times*, November 22):

I have escaped from that prison and I am never going back. School is finished anyway. There is no place in school for people who are committed to education.

The worship of the mechanical, which has itself produced some of our problems in the revolt of youth, was evidenced in the decision of the ILEA in 1972 not to have its annual Carol Service for 14,000 children at the Royal Festival Hall but to foster the "more liberated style of folk singing" by having a professional group singing on the TV network. The Authority wrote that thus "A larger number of children could be more effectively encouraged in their classrooms than in the Royal Festival Hall." The deputy head of Kidbrooke Park Junior School cut this fine talk down to size when she said:

Why must a carol concert be forward-looking? Carols are traditional, so what is wrong with children singing them as they have been sung for generations?

Visual and aural aids are only of use to a teacher if they are appropriate to the classroom situation. Any good teacher knows better than a producer what her particular children are prepared for and what excites them, and this will differ from year to year. The occasional special radio or television programme on biology, history or geography can help them, but it is rarely that a series will fit into a teacher's plans.

In school "chalk and talk" are still the most effective visual and aural aids, and the more equipment that is put into a classroom the more they are downgraded and the less time there is for them. The best infant schools are often those with least equipment. Put in a hall for drama and gymnastics, add a small playing-field for games, sand and water facilities, radio, television, video tape machines, tape recorders, and there will be no time for teaching reading since the teacher and the school are kept busy using all the facilities and the apparatus to justify the expenditure.

No, the cult of the visual aid is dead and the most deprived children are often those in schools with most equipment. Bring back the teacher to the centre of the stage and give him back his confidence.

PART III

Plan for Revival

Chapter 18

The Return of Authority

We shall not improve the quality of education in this country until we return to a sense of purpose, continuity and authority in our general attitude to life and society. We have witnessed an emphasis in our schools on purposeless creativity, a creativity based upon a false theory of personal self-sufficiency and undisciplined arrogance in place of painfully acquired wisdom. It is thus no wonder that there has been a crisis of purpose among so many university students.

Professor Duncan Williams, the author of *Trousered Apes*,* has pointed to the iconoclastic cleverness, emanating from an unanchored intellect which was the very quality Milton endowed Satan with—purposeless energy and rebellion—the ultimate in romanticism. As Duncan Williams also observes, Satan and his angels were imprisoned and not freed by their cleverness:

> To do aught good never will be our task
> But ever to do ill our sole delight,
> As being the contrary to his high will
> whom we resist.

It would appear that the progressives and the romantics have been similarly imprisoned by their opposition to order and structure.

The need for limits to be imposed or self-imposed on the

---

* Churchill Press, 1971.

desires and the wills of men has never been better expressed than by Edmund Burke in his *Reflections on the French Revolution*:

> Men are qualified for civil liberty in exact proportion to their disposition to put moral chains upon their appetites . . . Society cannot exist unless a controlling power upon will and appetite be placed somewhere, and the less of it there is within, the more there is without. It is ordained in the eternal constitution of things that men of intemperate minds cannot be free. Their passions forge their fetters.

We have betrayed young people by expecting them to develop their own personality and abilities at the same time as having to form for themselves a code of behaviour and a purpose for living. We have thrown away the spiritual and moral guiding-reins and wondered why youth has lost its way. The young of every species need to be trained for survival, and for human beings this includes the necessity of spiritual and moral training if they are not to destroy both themselves and others. A definite code of behaviour and of expectation helps them to develop true fulfilment within a framework of security.

We have seen the signs of destruction all around us. The *Children's Rights* publication of 1971 recommended sabotage to schoolchildren—"unscrew locks, smash tannoys, paint blackboards red, grind all chalk to dust". It was reported in 1974 that at Tulse Hill School under the ILEA, the efforts of the caring staff were "being ruined because some members of the staff are telling the boys that their chances of success in society as it exists today are nil". It is significant that most of the "group of extremist teachers, a dozen to 20" at that school, came from the English Department.

In the ILEA, also, attendance at adventure and play centres has been equated with proper learning at schools. In March 1974, it was reported that one such play centre at Vauxhall was on a wasteland site with nine organisers for some 30 children offering such activities as "impromptu music, dancing, dressing up, going to the cinema, lighting fires, painting and playing games", as if the children belonged to some wild nomadic tribe.

Further signs of breakdown in standards were seen in May 1972, when some few hundred children out of the 400,000 in ILEA schools walked out to take part in a Schools Action Union march against caning and uniforms, a march incited by outsiders in our age of fabricated grievances. Yet two heads of schools who took reasonably strong action against these political truants were rebuked in a letter from the Chief Education Officer which claimed that it was "important" to give "due consideration to the legitimate views of pupils, some of whom may have been involved in recent events". Once again, support for minority views representing some 1 in 1,000 pupils was used to undermine authority. The weakness of the last 25 years has been what Dr. W. H. Allchin has called, in another context, "a fearful evasion of responsibility".

The retreat of Dr. Spock from his "baby knows best" view, coinciding with an increasing concern of parents at large for standards and discipline, may signal a change of direction. This would be a return to the Arnoldian concept of a tradition of literature, art and ideas, which it is the responsibility of the cultured to maintain. This will necessitate a retreat from the value-free concept of the total social character of our society as represented by Albert Rowe, when he wrote that the new teacher "must recognise the working-class culture of pupils as valid. Not inferior to others, simply different". Of course, such working-class culture is "valid", but for the defence of civilisation and art it is inferior, like any form of middle-class culture, to high culture—the winnowed culture of the ages.

The teacher must again be trained to teach a body of knowledge within a dominant set of values. Children asking for bread must no longer be offered a stone. We must remember as a society that values are total and for all purposes. Dr. George Steiner even states that "an explicit grammar is an acceptance of order" and "the violent illiteracy of the graffiti of the modern counter-culture" . . . and "the nonsense cries of the stage 'happening' were the obvious opposition to this order".

The purpose of schools is to give such order, values and

guidance, while teaching skills and knowledge, and the purpose of universities is to seek for a fuller understanding of these values and objective truths. If schools and universities cease to fulfil these elevated purposes, there is no point in their continuance. They simply become an expensive exploitation of the rate- and taxpayer. We must therefore examine how schools and universities may return once more to their primary purposes.

Chapter 19

The Schools

The malaise in schools in Britain has followed from a breakdown in accepted curriculum and traditional values. There was little concern about either political control or parental choice so long as there was an "understood" curriculum which was followed by every school. Schools may have differed in efficiency but their common values or curriculum were broadly acceptable. The present disillusionment of parents arises from their resentment that their children's education now depends upon the lottery of the school to which they are directed. Standards decline because both measurement and comparisons are impossible when aims and curriculum become widely divergent.

These problems can be solved only by making schools again accountable to some authority outside them. The necessary sanction is either a nationally enforced curriculum or parental choice or a combination of both. It follows that there must also be a reassessment of teacher recruitment and training and of what can really be achieved in schooling.

It is not difficult to draw up a basic curriculum occupying some 60–80 per cent of teaching time in the infant, primary and secondary schools. All that would be necessary is the stipulation of standards in numeracy and basic literacy, geographical, historical and scientific knowledge to be attained at various ages by the average child. Achievement could then be monitored by nationally set and marked examinations, or by HMIs with increased power to visit the schools without warning and examine the children.

Government grants in the nineteenth century were dependent upon the standards attained in a school. Between 1862 and 1890 the grants were conditional upon the specific performance of individual children in the six standard examinations conducted by HMIs. One of the reasons for their introduction was the report of the Duke of Newcastle's Commission in 1861 that "the instruction given is commonly both too ambitious and too superficial in its character . . . and that it often omits to secure a thorough grounding in the simplest but most essential part of instruction".

This "payment by results" was less unpopular with teachers then than the low standard of schooling now is with parents, most of whom would echo the words of the Newcastle Commission. The Revised Code did improve reading standards because teachers had to concentrate on skills and not on indoctrination.

There could surely be a middle way whereby the basic attainments of children were tested at the ages of seven, 11 and 14. Such examinations would re-establish public confidence.

Both the Labour and Conservative parties have moved towards the return of some form of national standards. A Labour Party policy statement of 1973 stipulated:

If the pupils of a particular school consistently fall short of the normal achievements for their age group, the local authority must be required to make proposals for remedying the defect.

The Department of Education announced in August 1974, that it would establish a new department to assess the performance of children in school and identify the extent of under-achievement. At that time Norman St. John-Stevas, the Conservative education spokesman, said that the Conservatives proposed to provide tests which would be carried out in schools by an expanded and strengthened school inspectorate. He added:

We would thus provide teachers with objective targets . . . We want to ensure that children are able to do basic mathematics, to read easily, to have a good command of English and to express themselves in writing.

Such defence of nationally examined standards as a reaction against the extremes of progressive thought has already begun to affect the schools. Dr. Joyce Morris made a blistering attack on nonsensical advice on reading at the North of England Education Conference in January 1975. The School Mathematics Project, one of the major modern mathematics schemes, was recently changed to include more repetitive drills to provide practice in arithmetical skills.

In California there are mandatory testing programmes for different grade levels and the results are published in newspapers. There have also been experiments in the United States with "performance contracting" whereby firms specialising in teaching undertake to achieve certain standards with children of set abilities and are only paid if they attain them. Some 150 experiments in performance contracting have been supported by the Office of Economic Opportunity and in Gary, Indiana, one set of contractors even took over a school. It is doubtful, however, whether such contracting would be necessary in Britain if the standards attained by schools with all children were regularly examined.

The movement to compulsory comprehensive schools and the Labour Party's hostility to all forms of independent education have revived the great debate about to whom children "belong" and the right of parents to make decisions about how their children should be educated. The growth of collectivism and state power in the West, as well as in the Eastern bloc and China, has moved the balance away from the individual. The logical outcome was embraced by Professor F. Musgrove when he wrote in *The Family Education and Society* in 1966:

It is the business of education to eliminate the influence of parents. We have decided that children shall no longer be at the mercy of their parents and it is the business of local education authorities to see that they are not.

This contrasts strongly with the statement of John Stuart Mill a century earlier:

A general state education is a mere contrivance for making people to be exactly like one another.

Yet there is international acceptance of the rights of parents which are now denied by the Labour Party in the United Kingdom. Clause 26, part 3 of the United Nations Covenant on Human rights states, "The parents have a prior right to choose the kind of education that shall be given to their children." Article 2 of protocol 1 of the European Human Rights Conference which the British government ratified in 1951 states:

The state shall respect the right of parents to ensure . . . education and teaching in conformity with their own religious and philosophical convictions.

How can such guarantees be squared with the mounting threats against independent and direct grant schools of the United Kingdom by the Labour Party over the last few years? Roy Hattersley, then Labour education spokesman, said in 1973,

I must leave you with no doubts about our serious intention to reduce and eventually to abolish private education in this country.

Apart from Hitler's proscription of Kurt Hahn's (the founder of Gordonstoun) Salem, the only example modern Europe affords of a prohibition and expropriation of independent schools is Emile Combes' attempt to close the Jesuit Schools in France in 1903.

The charge is made by Labour Party spokesmen that not only are independent schools divisive but they are overstaffed. Of course all freedom and diversity can be described as "divisive", but the criticism that they are overstaffed—and so take more than their fair share of teachers—is just not true. The public schools' staffing ratio of 1:12 seems modest compared with ILEA's 1:14·6 in secondary schools, when allowance is made for their 24-hour boarding needs. Some state sixth-form colleges have staffing ratios of 1:11 and 1:11·5 and a high proportion of public school boys are sixth formers who are much more demanding in teacher time.

The Labour Party's indignation about independent education has no doubt been intensified by sourness over their unexpected success over the last fifteen years. It was confidently anticipated in the late 1950s that state schools would become ever more successful, that fewer parents would therefore be prepared to pay fees, and that the public schools would conveniently wither away. Instead, the fall in disciplinary and academic standards along with the march of compulsory comprehensive schools since the mid-1960s has rudely ended this expectation. Between 1946 and 1971, preparatory, independent and public schools catering for some 5 per cent of the school population have increased their enrolment by 46 per cent, and are now increasing by some 3–5 per cent a year. Even in the face of the Labour Party's threats, £23 million was spent on new buildings, improvements and new equipment by independent schools in 1973.

Selection, motivation, the demands of the Common Entrance Examination and external examinations at 16 and 18, have all helped to keep up the standards of independent schools. The 174 direct grant schools, which receive direct government grants in return for making one-quarter of their places available to parents who cannot afford fees, are also academically superb. Some 56·6 per cent of their pupils obtained two 'A' levels and 32 per cent won university places in 1969. Direct grant schools are a link between the state and the independent system. They also offer wide opportunities to boys from a variety of social backgrounds. Figures are available from Queen Elizabeth Hospital School,

Bristol, comparing the occupations of parents with the national distribution of occupations on the 1966 General Register of Occupations.

	Queen Elizabeth Hospital School Parents Occupation %	1966 Gen. Register of Occupations	Boarding wing of Q.E. School Parents Occupation
Professional (1)	7	11	6
Intermediate (2)	15	24	26
Skilled (3)	46	53	50
Semi-skilled (4)	25	7	10
Unskilled (5)	7	5	8

The head of this school has pointed out that parental occupations are even closer to the national pattern when allowance is made for various distortions. Thus parents on the school forms tend to upgrade their occupations from postman to civil servant, unskilled to skilled engineer and so on, while some left-wing heads of primary schools may not put their boys in for free places because, on political grounds, they prefer them to attend the local comprehensive school.

The two Reports of the Public Schools Commission were contradictory on direct grant and public schools. The first Report (1968) chaired by Sir John Newson, recommended the integration of the public schools into the national state system and suggested that half of their places should, within seven years, go to pupils from state schools. The second Report (1970) chaired by Professor David Donnison, recommended that all direct grant schools should go independent or else become comprehensive within the state system.

Meanwhile, other Western countries have independent schools. In Australia they cater for 22 per cent of all pupils, in New Zealand 15·5 per cent, in the USA 10 per cent, in the Federal Republic of Germany 15 per cent and in France 20 per cent.

It is doubtful if independent schools could be prohibited in

Britain, unless we moved much closer to an authoritarian society. Aneurin Bevan wrote in 1955:

> I do not favour private education, but I would not prohibit it, provided the welfare of the children is safeguarded by state inspection.

It would certainly be a strange Britain where hard drugs, hard pornography and private schooling were the only prohibitions. One would foresee a situation where private tutors moved from house to house under cover of darkness and were concealed in "teacher holes" like the priest holes of the seventeenth century. Would parents also be prohibited from spending their money on BBC2 sets, books, paintings, quality magazines and theatre visits which might give their children an "unfair" advantage? A society which prohibited parental sacrifice so that they could improve the quality of their children's education, while they were encouraged to spend money on family holidays on the Costa Brava or visits to hooligan-controlled soccer matches, would have lost all claim to the moral allegiance of its subjects.

A Labour Party, that claimed the right of conscientious objection when the Engineers Union opposed the Industrial Relations Court, then the law of the land, could hardly object to parents defying a state law which prohibited private education. The speech of Mr. Wedgwood Benn, MP, in favour of the engineers' union could be thrown back at the Labour Party by these parents:

> Conscientious objection is well understood in Britain and is respected, even in wartime when the very survival of the nation is at stake ... Conscientious belief led some of the finest people to challenge man-made law and they have thus established our right to the liberties we enjoy.

The Plowden Report argued that one of the essentials for educational improvement was a closer partnership between schools and parents. Such a partnership obviously occurs in independent schools, if only because a parent chooses a school whose values are the same as the home and the pupil is well aware of this agreement. A similar relationship can be taken for granted in state schools when pupils are successful in the 11-plus grammar school selection examination and parents are given a choice of school. It does not occur when pupils are directed to a neighbourhood comprehensive school which parents dislike. Nor can we expect an harmonious partnership when progressive parents are directed to send their son to a traditional neighbourhood primary school, or in the more frequent cases when traditional parents are directed to send their son to the progressive neighbourhood primary school.

The 1944 Education Act attempted to balance the advantages of parental choice against its costs. It stipulated that local education authorities should have regard to "the general principle that . . . pupils are to be educated in accordance with the wishes of their parents . . . as far as it is compatible with the provision of efficient instruction . . . and the avoidance of unreasonable public expenditure".

It would seem obvious that a free society would move to more, not less, parental choice of school with advancing standards of living. Indeed, a 1970 survey commissioned by the Institute of Economic Affairs, showed that 55 per cent of parents would be prepared to contribute towards the education of their children if they were allowed a choice and some remission of taxation. With direct contributions parents believed that they would have more say in the form of education chosen for their children.

The best way to obtain this choice would certainly not be by further enforcement of comprehensive schooling but by helping parents to buy the education they want by replacing state provision with a reverse income tax or the educational voucher. All schools would then have to meet the demands of enough parents to fill their places or be reduced in size, closed or taken over. There would be a variety of schools to satisfy the differing demands of parents as there are shops and suppliers to match the preferences of other consumers.

The *American Left* moved to support the educational voucher because of the collapse of city ghetto schools and they see the voucher as giving opportunity whereas the English Libertarian Right see the voucher as giving choice. Since schools would expand and contract, open and close, according to their ability to meet the demand, there would be little need of state control beyond the enforcement of certain minimum standards. The popularity with parents would be the real test of a school's efficiency.

There is little doubt that the introduction of the voucher in Britain would mean a rapid expansion of independent education. The emergence of the free school movement; the Independent Open School, which provides tutors for pupils in their homes; and the attempts in 1972 and 1973 by Islington parents to operate their own traditional school, have shown how widespread is the demand for radical change of the state system.

Sir Robert Lowe, who coined the celebrated sentence, "We must compel our future Masters to learn their letters", after the 1867 extension of the franchise, also said:

Parents have one great superiority over the government or the administration . . . their faults are mainly the corrigible faults of ignorance, not of apathy and prejudice. They have and feel the greatest interest in doing that which is for the benefit of their children.

It is possible that a combination of enforced minimim national standards tested by HMIs combined with the voucher and parental choice would be best for British education. John Stuart Mill emphasised that what mattered was the educational standards reached, not the length of schooling, and enforced minimum standards would guarantee these basic standards while the competition for excellence in schools to win parental choice would lift them higher.

In Denmark any 85 parents who agree on a project can set up a school and gain the support of the state. This is really a form of simplified voucher arrangement since parents are given by the state the means of financing the education of their children.

Belgium and the Netherlands have somewhat similar arrangements.

There have been several battles between the local education
authorities and individual parents over school attendance. In the
course of a 10-year struggle from 1952–62, Mrs. J. Baker was
fined twice, was sentenced to two months imprisonment and her
children were made and unmade wards of court. Only after 10
years did a Court of Appeal find, as Mrs. Baker had always
maintained, that she was giving her children an education that
was "suitable" for them in the terms of the 1944 Act. In 1972
Kenneth Sibley of Luton was sent to prison when he insisted that
his daughters should attend a grammar school, and there have
been numerous cases of Moslem parents refusing to send their
girls to mixed schools. It is likely, with the advance of comprehensive schools, that such cases will increase.

Schemes like sixth form colleges and community schools are
only of marginal importance to the deep-seated educational issues
which centre on parental choice, educational standards and
whether progressive education and comprehensive schools are
successful or whether schools should return to traditional teaching
schemes and forms of selection. The sixth-form college could
help to maintain standards where sixth forms are small in comprehensive schools, provided the colleges have tight academic
standards and are selective in intake. There were some 50 sixth
form colleges approved or in operation by mid-1974. But Mrs.
Thatcher, as Secretary of State at the DES, preferred the traditional sixth form and the AMA has pointed out that well-qualified
teachers, particularly graduates, hesitate to accept posts at schools
with no sixth form work. This could mean lower standards in the
11–16 schools.

The move to comprehensive schools which attempt to give all
pupils a similar non-streamed, equal-subject education has come
at a very strange time. Up to the post-Second World War period,
the white collar worker had considerable advantages in both
income and security of tenure compared with the unskilled,
semi-skilled and even skilled worker. This is no longer the case
and the market is now rewarding the young manual worker with
money and security often more generously than the white-collar

worker. It is thus no wonder that many non-academic boys resent the raising of the school-leaving age which keeps them from well-paid employments, while the academically-gifted boy resents the slower intellectual pace of comprehensive schools which hinder his self-fulfilment.

Community schools, which embrace local facilities and which adults also attend in the evening and even in the daytime, may help to generate community interest in a school. They are based on the Henry Morris Cambridgeshire Village College concept and they have been introduced in towns like Blackburn where the schools also provide the local libraries, clinics and swimming pools. However, according to *Parents and Schools* (the Newsletter of the Confederation for the Advancement of State Education) such schools create much bickering between the day school, the adult classes, the youth centre and other users. This could perhaps be avoided by the appointment of a an overall Principal advised by a directly-elected local committee.

The quality of teachers is crucial to schools. Low standards of entry, poor training and life-tenure have not helped. Higher standards of entry could be demanded now that a falling birth-rate has lessened the demand for teachers. A College training should be preceded by one year's pupil-teacher apprenticeship attached to a capable teacher, thereby ensuring that college entrants had the necessary mental and physical stamina for teaching. A two-year College of Education course could then be offered, leading to a licensed diploma and the third year could be supervised school teaching. Lecturers at the College of Education should be heads and teachers from schools on five-year secondments. A sabbatical term in every five years could be offered to teachers to revise their own subjects, and a staff college opened to which all teachers go for a month's or a term's course whenever they were promoted to head of house or year or department, and again on promotion to head or deputy head. As at Colleges of Education, the tutors would be heads and staff on secondment, and visits would also be made to schools.

Finally the compulsory school leaving age should be reduced to 14 or 15 years again. Pupils should be allowed to leave at this age subject to a number of conditions: firstly that their parents and school agreed; secondly that they had passed a 14-plus minimum level national examination; thirdly, that they have an attendance record of at least 95 per cent over the three previous years; and finally that they have a job to go to. If they became genuinely unemployed for two to four weeks before their sixteenth birthday, they could be taken back into full-time education. These requirements would mean that it paid a boy to gain the 14-plus examination standard and many would then be more advanced at the age of 14 than they are now at the age of 16. Many having made the effort to qualify for leaving may then decide to stay on. The threat of return to school if they lost their job would also help boys and girls to choose their employment more wisely and to settle down. A little more common sense realism and a little less intellectual dreaming would help to transform the British educational system.

Chapter 20

Higher Education and Universities

The threat to university standards and academic freedom in the early 1970s was a product of over-rapid expansion and the granting of a free ride to students irrespective of their motivation. It became the accepted view that just as middle-class and aspiring working-class parents expected their children to pass the 11-plus, so they would henceforth automatically expect their 18-year olds to go as of right to university, whether or not the young people themselves were keen. The remarkable point about the student explosion is not that there were troubles at universities but they were not more widespread and more pronounced when many students did not even know what they were supposed to be doing in higher education.

The best way to test motivation of students is probably by a partial or full loan system. A commitment to repay part of the very high costs of tuition and maintenance will cause the 18-year old to pause and weigh up whether he really wants to go on to higher education. The Robbins Report of 1963 dismissed loans in two and a half pages on the rather flimsy grounds that what it chose to call the "habit" of going up to university, particularly among women and the poor, was not sufficiently established to withstand any discouragement. The report added:

> . . . if as time goes on, the habit is more freely established, the arguments of justice in distribution and of the advantage of increasing individual responsibility may come to weigh more heavily and lead to some experiment in this direction.

It is thus of special significance that by 1971 Lord Robbins wrote (*Financial Times*, 21st August):

> I venture to suggest that the time has now come when those who receive support for higher education should be required to make some repayment thereof if it results in identifiable material advantage.

In January 1972 it was reported that the Department of Education and Science had drawn up a plan to replace student maintenance grants in part by a loan scheme. The 1974 Parliamentary Select Committee Inquiry into Postgraduate Education recommended not only a cut in the number of post-graduate students but a loan system to maintain them. In the same year an independent group of academics convened by Professor Roy Niblett of London University, urged a partial loan system for all students.

As long as higher education is free and maintenance grants are also given, subject only to a parental means test, there is no real test of motivation. The Colleges of Education have become the girls' finishing schools of the twentieth century, maintained at public expense. It could be argued that if all such Colleges achieve is to make women better mothers, then it is the 15-plus leaver from a deprived home and not the 18-plus leaver from a satisfactory home who should enjoy this experience.

The Robbins Report did not refute other evidence that a university degree and higher education often is a means whereby middle and artisan working-class children increase their personal income at the expense of the more poorly-endowed families in the community who help to finance it. In Denmark, the annual rate of return for higher education has been calculated at 10 per cent on the cost in most occupations. Estimates by Becker in the USA put the personal return on higher education as high as 13–14 per cent, a figure supported by Professor Mark Blaug in the UK. Redistributive justice would suggest that better maintenance grants for

16–18-year-olds who stay on at school from low income families would be more just than free higher education places.

It is thus no wonder that most countries have some form of loans in addition to public subsidies for higher education students. Denmark gives approximately half of its help to students by way of loans from the state or by government-guaranteed loans from private banks. Finland and Norway have loan schemes and Sweden also gives more than half of its help by way of loans. Special arrangements are invariably made where there are difficulties in repaying—which does not prove a large problem—and not only are there few defaulters, but graduates who emigrate continue repaying for their education from abroad.

Evidence from Europe indicates that loans do not deter working-class or women applicants. A Danish study showed that the proportion of women students has risen as loans have become more widespread, and in Norway the average woman who has benefited from higher education returns part of the benefit by working 20 years. Loans are not unknown in the UK. The Bell Educational Trust, which runs three foreign language schools, proposed a scheme in 1973 for £600 loans for students taking intensive six-month courses. The National Westminster Bank also made £150,000 available for £900 loans, at 4 per cent interest for the first three years and $2\frac{1}{2}$ per cent over bank rate for the next seven years, to postgraduate management students.

The USA has a highly-developed loans system. Aid to low-income families is given by way of subsidised loans. Commercial and private banks provide a large proportion of these funds, which are guaranteed by government and have a below-market interest rate.

There have been suggestions in the UK of a graduate tax as developed by Professor Prest, whereby graduates earning above a certain level pay more tax. It is not always made clear whether such special payments would continue when a graduate has paid back a set proportion or indeed all of the cost of his degree to the state. It would also mean that graduates who joined lower-paid professions, like teaching, would pay no extra tax so that their employers would be indirectly subsidisd.

It might be a reasonable compromise for government to cover

approved capital costs and perhaps half the running costs of universities, on condition that fees were raised to cover the balance. The fees and realistic living costs could then be covered by loans. This would mean that each student would consider the usefulness of any course he contemplated, weighing the cost against likely future earnings. A student would have to be genuinely committed if he borrowed for a course which did not promise to butter his bread. Each potential student would also weigh up the financial advantages of living at home, whereas on the present grants system everyone is encouraged to enjoy living away at someone else's expense. If a generous upper limit was fixed, it would be for each student to decide how he lived at university and how much he borrowed.

To keep scholarship alive, some 10,000 national scholarships could be given every year, on a liberal basis, to the students who gained the highest marks at 'A' level irrespective of what they studied at university. The brightest academically would thus be granted higher education while for the rest there would be a direct test of personal motivation. There would be no longer the automatic escalator carrying passive passengers on to university and other higher education.

Such a system might certainly mean that there would be a reduction in higher education numbers and institutions from the present 44 universities and 30 polytechnics. The Colleges of Education in which neither the students nor the schools have much faith would have to change or close down. If the number and size of universities declined they would return to what universities were intended to be, namely nurseries for high achievers and retreats for scholars. Dr. G. S. Brosan, Principal of the N.E. London Polytechnic said in 1970: "Universities stand for the nurturing of apprentice scholars; polytechnics for the nurturing of apprentice industrialists." This vision would divide higher education into its various specialities and put an end to all the talk of "comprehensive universities".

On the issue of specialisation in higher education, it should be recalled that one neglected proposal of the Robbins Report was increased specialisation. It suggested that eight centres of scientific and technical excellence should be established, five new and

three developed from existing institutions. In the prevailing egalitarian climate, it is hardly surprising that this recommendation
was ignored. Instead, the higher education establishments pro-
ducing technologists were increased so that, allowing for population, the UK would have 40 per cent more technologists than
the USA!

One great advantage of loans would be that it would really
bring the market into education. They would make the creation
and blossoming of independent non-state institutions, like the
Independent University at Buckingham, much more likely. More
students might also then enrol with the Open University, which
catered for "second-chance" scholars at an average current and
capital cost between one-third and one-sixth of the level at the
conventional universities. We would then see the extent of state
subventions necessary for the Open University to compete with
correspondence courses preparing for external degrees.

A major advantage of loans would be that, by diversifying the
sources of finance, universities would enjoy wider freedom from
dependence on state control. It is significant that Clive Jenkins,
the secretary of ASTMS, attacked the Independent University as
a threat to the collectivist and egalitarian philosophy.

Loans would also correct an anomaly in education created by
the reduction of the age of majority to 18. Under present arrangements a student is considered an independent adult at the age of
18 and yet his parents are held responsible for maintaining him at
university. This parental contribution towards his living costs and
fees is calculated on a parental means test although it cannot be
enforced against parents who refuse to pay it and their children
are not reimbursed by the state or the local education authority.
This parental contribution is widely resented by both parents and
students. Assessed parental contributions as a percentage of the
total student grants rose from 17·2 per cent in 1962 to some 30
per cent in 1972. An indication of the number of parents who
refuse to make up the grant can be gained from a survey of
Edinburgh students which showed that 20 per cent of home-
based students and 50 per cent of students away from home did not
have their full grant made up by their parents. On average students
were between £3 and £4 a week short of their full allowance.

The difficulties of the parental contribution may make students more inclined to support a loan system. In principle, most students consider such loans to be just but incline to favour their introduction the year after they graduate! A survey at University College, Swansea, found that a quarter of the students would be prepared to pay part of their accommodation and subsistence costs and one-eighth would pay the full cost.

A gap between school and higher education would be another test of student motivation. It would also help increase the maturity of students. The post-Second World War ex-service entry to British universities achieved outstanding results—and many countries have moved towards the recruitment of students of greater maturity.

Maoist China expects its university students to have done several years hard labour in the armed services or in agriculture before they enter university. Students are given extra money for each additional year they have been engaged in outside labour. It may be this greater maturity which allows China to have a training period for secondary school teachers of only one and a half years. Russia also encourages outside experience before students enter university and these mature students sit an easier examination for university entry.

The UK only gave 30 mature scholarships in 1973 for those over 25 years, although one in every ten students entering university the previous year was of this age. Lord Robbins in his article in the *Financial Times* (August 1971), moved to the support of a gap between school and university when he wrote:

The rule I propose is that there should be no grant or advances for a fixed period after school leaving. I have little doubt that, were it adopted, there would be less infirmity of purpose, far more appreciation of the privilege of the receipt of higher education than there is at present.

It is certainly worth considering the introduction of a system where grants were only given or loans offered on favourable terms after a two or three year period from leaving school. Even on commercial calculations, a student putting down £1,000 deposit from his own earnings would be a much better risk with a smaller chance of defaulting on his loan repayment.

Firm action must also be taken to safeguard academic freedom and debate, although a reduction of numbers in higher education, and the emphasis on loans and more mature students would all help. The freedom of university debate must be based upon the principle of reciprocity which was brought out by John Locke in his "Letter Concerning Toleration", where he insisted that toleration could not then be offered to Roman Catholics because they would not allow reciprocal liberty if they came to power. No one should be allowed into university who does not accept the reciprocity of free speech and disclaim all physical force, violence and harassment.

Commenting on the Annan Report on Essex University, Mr. Jo Grimond, MP, observed that the cumbersome disciplinary procedures laid down by the Privy Council handicapped universities when dealing with disruptive students. Elaborate procedures simply lead to more trouble.

A pledge of good behaviour could be demanded from each student before he joined a university and he should sign the acceptance of a simple rule book. Mr. Charles Carter, the Vice-Chancellor of Lancaster University, attempted in April 1972, to enforce a pledge of good behaviour each term before allowing students to draw their grant cheques. Unfortunately, despite the support of Sir William Alexander, the secretary of the Association of Education Committees, he was let down by the individual local education authorities who would have had to agree to withhold grants on the advice of the university.

The cause of most of the trouble in Britain is the automatic financing of the student unions which all students have to join. In 1971 this became a matter of great debate. A document published by the Department of Education and Science suggested a choice of possible reforms: firstly, that a registrar should supervise expenditure of the unions; secondly, that the grant to student unions should come from the block grant to the individual universities; and thirdly, that membership of student unions should be voluntary and the financing of sporting facilities should be taken over by the university. The Parliamentary Select Committee on Estimates and the Federation of Conservative Students preferred the first suggestion, the government favoured the second, and the general public would probably have welcomed the third. Since the second suggestion would have brought each University Senate into regular conflict with its student union, it is little wonder that the Vice-Chancellors as well as the students opposed it. The result was that nothing was done and the issue was postponed once again.

In a free society there is no reason why membership of student unions should be compulsory. It would be better if the £10–30 per student now paid to the student unions by the local education authorities were given directly to the student. Sporting and cultural facilities could be provided by the universities and each student would be free to decide for himself whether he would join his union or not. This would end the pernicious system where large sums of money are almost automatically provided for an irresponsible minority of student agitators.

In the last resort, however, the defence of university standards and freedoms will depend upon the convictions, integrity and courage of the University Vice-Chancellors and teachers. It will also depend upon the climate of national and international opinion and whether an age which stresses equality leaves room for liberty, without which equality is a purposeless pursuit.

This liberty of thought is indeed under threat when 50 eminent scientists, including three Nobel prizewinners, were moved to declare in 1972 that "published positions are often misquoted and misrepresented; emotional appeals replace scientific reasoning, arguments are directed against the man rather than against the evidence".

That such a statement was necessary in the university world shows that we not only face increasing illiteracy but that we are faced with a threat of thought and speech repression which would herald a new dark age. This is the true crisis in education against which we must react.